# What Teachers Need to Know About Language

Edited by
Carolyn Temple Adger, Catherine E. Snow, and Donna Christian

Printed in the United States of America
10 9 8 7 6 5 4 3 2 1

**Language in Education: Theory and Practice 97**

Copyediting and production supervision: Jeanne Rennie
Editorial assistance: Amy Fitch
Production, design, and cover: SAGARTdesign

**ISBN 1-887744-75-4**

This publication was made possible in part by a grant from Carnegie Corporation of New York to Harvard University. The statements made and views expressed are solely the responsibility of the authors.

Partial funding for this publication was provided by the National Library of Education in the U.S. Department of Education's Office of Educational Research and Improvement under contract no. ED-99-CO-0008 to the Center for Applied Linguistics. The opinions expressed do not necessarily reflect the positions or policies of the Department of Education.

**Library of Congress Cataloging-in-Publication Data**

What teachers need to know about language / edited by Carolyn Temple Adger, Catherine E. Snow, and Donna Christian ; prepared by ERIC Clearinghouse on Languages and Linguistics.
        p. cm. — (Language in education ; 97)
Includes bibliographical references.
      ISBN 1-887744-75-4 (alk. paper)
   1.   Linguistic minorities—Education—United States. 2.   Children of minorities—Education—United States. 3.   Teachers—In-service training—United States. 4.   Language and education—United States.   I. Adger, Carolyn Temple. II. Snow, Catherine E. III. Christian, Donna. IV. ERIC Clearinghouse on Languages and Linguistics. V. Series.

LC3728.W43 2002
371.102'2—dc21

2002031246

# What Teachers Need to Know About Language

Edited by
Carolyn Temple Adger, Catherine E. Snow, and Donna Christian

A publication of Delta Systems Co., Inc., and The Center for Applied Linguistics
Prepared by the ERIC Clearinghouse on Languages and Linguistics

# Acknowledgments

The editors thank Jodi Crandall, Doug Demo, Susan Hoyle, Joy Kreeft Peyton, Jennie Pilato, and Jeannie Rennie for thoughtful discussions during the preparation of this book.

# Table of Contents

# Introduction

This book represents a conversation among educators and others concerned with language and literacy development. The conversation began by chance at an international conference on literacy when Catherine Snow and Lily Wong Fillmore began talking about the escalating demands that the educational system in the United States places on teachers without giving them the support they need to meet those demands. Snow had just chaired a National Research Council committee on Prevention of Reading Difficulties in Young Children that focused on what teachers need to know to provide children with the opportunities that they deserve to learn to read. Surveying teacher education programs across the country, the committee found that few programs provided the depth and breadth of information that committee members felt was needed. At the same time, Fillmore had been pressing for more attention to language and literacy in teacher education. Clearly, the two scholars agreed, teachers need more knowledge about these domains than teacher education programs typically provide. They decided to develop a paper laying out their views and circulate it to colleagues for comment.

That paper—the first draft of this volume's focal chapter, "What Teachers Need to Know About Language"—came to the attention of Carol Rasco, who at that time worked in the Office of Educational Research and Improvement (OERI) in the U.S. Department of Education. Rasco persuaded

Snow and Fillmore to expand the paper and to develop a workshop that would help educators think creatively about some of the issues raised in the paper. The particular issue addressed in the workshop was how to think about language and literacy, which can be hard, especially for educators who themselves had no difficulty acquiring language and literacy skills. Good readers may find it difficult to understand why someone else would have trouble reading. Snow and Fillmore conducted their workshop in 1999 at three regional conferences on Improving America's Schools organized by the U.S. Department of Education. Practitioners' questions and comments there expanded the conversation. A composite videotape and viewers' guide, *Why Reading Is Hard*, were developed to bring the conference workshop to those involved in the professional development of teachers (www.WhyReadingIsHard.com).

## Perspectives on Teachers' Knowledge About Language

Centered on Fillmore and Snow's paper, this volume adds voices to the conversation about what teachers need to know about language. Chapter 1 is a revised version of the original Fillmore and Snow paper. The revisions were made in response to readers' comments and questions on earlier versions. In subsequent chapters, we invited colleagues from several educational domains to comment on the first chapter and to discuss implications of Fillmore and Snow's arguments for the particular area in which they work.

This volume begins then with Fillmore and Snow's exposition on the language knowledge that all teachers need. The authors argue that teachers need a depth and breadth of expertise about language because of the range of functions they must serve. As communicators with students from diverse backgrounds, teachers need to understand that structural differences among languages and contrasting cultural patterns for language use may well affect their students' discourse. In their role as educators, teachers need to know how English proficiency develops in native speakers and in speakers who are learning English as a second language. Understanding language development and acquisition helps teachers select appropriate materials for their students. Similarly, fulfilling their role as evaluators means knowing what language behaviors to expect based on students' language backgrounds, so as not to confuse predictable dialect and language learning features with language delay. Teachers are also expected to know about language by virtue of their role as educated human beings, and to contribute this information to discussions in schools and beyond. Finally, teachers are important agents of socialization, who support children's developing identities as students and who help children from backgrounds that contrast with schools' expectations learn to function comfortably in another language and culture.

Having established this functional rationale for their argument, Fillmore and Snow outline what teachers should know about language in terms of questions they should be able to answer and relate to their classroom practice. The first set of questions focuses on oral language:

- What are the basic units of language?
- What's regular and what isn't?
- How is the lexicon acquired and structured?
- Are vernacular dialects different from "bad English" and, if so, how?
- What is academic English?
- Why has the acquisition of English by non-English-speaking children not been more universally successful?

The second set concerns written language:

- Why is English spelling so complicated?
- Why do some children have more trouble than others in developing early reading skills?
- Why do students have trouble with structuring narrative and expository writing?
- How should one judge the quality and correctness of a piece of writing?
- What makes a sentence or a text easy or difficult to understand?

The chapter's final section lists courses or course components that would help teachers answer these questions: Language and Linguistics, Language and Cultural Diversity, Sociolinguistics for Educators in a Linguistically Diverse Society, Language Development, Second Language Learning and Teaching, The Language of Academic Discourse, and Text Analysis and Language Understanding in Educational Settings.

In the second chapter, "Language and Early Childhood Programs," Sue Bredekamp, Director of Research at the Council for Early Childhood Professional Recognition, applauds Fillmore and Snow's vision of teacher knowledge. She also explains why it seems unattainable for teachers of preschool children. Despite research evidence of the potential for high-quality early childhood education programs to prevent later school failure, particularly if a strong emphasis is placed on language development, this advantage is not available to all children because there are too few high-quality programs. Early childhood programs are often staffed by teachers with minimal qualifications, and there is high turnover because teachers are poorly paid. As things stand, concludes Bredekamp, it is unlikely that teachers in early childhood programs will be able to develop the full array of knowledge about language that they need.

Two commentaries from teacher educators agree with Bredekamp and with each other that Fillmore and Snow have outlined teacher knowledge that is crucial to improving education in a diverse society. Both emphasize, however, that adding new courses to teacher education curricula is simply impossible, no matter how essential the body of knowledge. The authors propose some possible solutions to this problem. In chapter 3, "Educating Teachers About Language," Leonard Baca and Kathy Escamilla suggest including language and literacy study throughout the undergraduate and graduate curriculum, as well as in in-service training. In chapter 4, "Teacher Knowledge About Language," Virginia Richardson suggests new ways to contextualize the foundational knowledge identified by Fillmore and Snow. It might be used in professional development programs to help determine what practical knowledge teaching demands. Pursuing a set of themes that are close to classroom practice and that cut across many foundational areas could bring together formal and practical knowledge about language.

In chapter 5, "Incorporating Linguistic Knowledge in Standards for Teacher Performance," Donna M. Gollnick of the National Council for Accreditation of Teacher Education (NCATE) shows similarities among Fillmore and Snow's dimensions of knowledge about language, those in the standards developed by two professional associations, and those in NCATE's standards for teaching. Echoing the two previous chapters on the impossibility of simply tinkering with the teacher education curriculum, Gollnick points out that

teacher preparation programs might adopt NCATE's focus on teacher performance rather than on course requirements to assess what teachers know
about language.

Promoting language development among English language learners concerns
all of the authors. Gollnick also emphasizes Fillmore and Snow's discussion of
dialect awareness for teachers, as does Sandra Feldman, President of the
American Federation of Teachers (AFT), in chapter 6, "Preparing Teachers to
Guide Children's Language Development." Knowledge about variation in
English is crucial for promoting Standard English development in speakers of
other dialects. Feldman adds that pedagogy must be culturally responsive, cap-
italizing on students' cultural backgrounds rather than overriding or negating
them. Her chapter also emphasizes the AFT's longstanding concern with literacy instruction. In a recent publication entitled, appropriately enough,
*Teaching Reading IS Rocket Science* (AFT, 1999), the AFT calls for reform of
teacher preparation and professional development to ensure that teachers
know how to teach reading to all children, particularly to English language
learners and vernacular English speakers.

The epilogue to this volume, by Catherine Snow, revisits the first chapter in
light of the subsequent ones and lists several national teacher education
reform efforts that may contribute to improving the linguistic education of
the nation's teachers.

## Shared Foci

Several themes cut across the commentaries on Fillmore and Snow's chapter.
All of the authors agree that deeper knowledge on the part of teachers about
language, linguistics (especially sociolinguistics), and language learning and
development—that is, educational linguistics—is vital to better education for
U.S. students. At present, many teachers are under-prepared to help their students develop the language and literacy skills they need to succeed in school
and careers.

The practical realities of changing teacher education, however, are very much
on the minds of the commentary writers whose work is driven by state limits on course work, university traditions, standards, and licensing exams.

Feldman points to another important curb on incorporating educational linguistics into teacher preparation: Most teacher education departments do not have faculty to teach the prescribed content, and faculty in the arts and sciences may not be interested in developing courses for teachers. Baca and Escamilla point out that expanding linguistic knowledge for teachers can't be delegated solely to teacher education: Attending to language must be taken up elsewhere in higher education and in K–12 schools, as Fillmore and Snow assert. The energy with which the commentaries discuss barriers to changing the education of teachers seems to reflect the climate of criticism and frustration surrounding the current focus on teacher quality, a particularly sensitive dimension of the demand for educational reform. Everyone wants good schools, but making changes anywhere in the vast educational enterprise exposes deeply rooted, interwoven constraints.

Explicating the challenge of altering teacher education, each commentary also discusses possibilities for making changes. Chapter authors agree with Fillmore and Snow that the standards initiatives of states and professional associations—standards for students' learning and standards for teaching—offer a potent opportunity. Because the standards represent some level of consensus, because some sets of standards are tied to testing, and because standards are associated with change, they may provide an opening for enhancing learning about language. Furthermore, as Gollnick and Feldman show, there is congruence between the Fillmore and Snow work and several associations' standards. So whatever is being done to meet those standards provides a natural home for implementing Fillmore and Snow's recommendations.

Carolyn Temple Adger, Washington, DC
Catherine E. Snow, Cambridge, MA
Donna Christian, Washington, DC

May 25, 2001

# Reference

American Federation of Teachers. (1999). *Teaching reading IS rocket science: What expert teachers of reading should know and be able to do.* Washington, DC: AFT Educational Issues Publications.

# Chapter One

# What Teachers Need to Know About Language

Lily Wong Fillmore, University of California at Berkeley
Catherine E. Snow, Harvard Graduate School of Education

Today's teachers need access to a wide range of information to function well in the classroom. The competencies required by the various state certification standards add up to a very long list indeed. Perhaps because this list is so long, teacher preparation programs often do not make time for substantial attention to crucial matters, choosing instead a checklist approach to addressing the various required competencies.

The challenge of providing excellent teacher preparation and ongoing professional development for teachers is enormous at any time. At a time like this, when the nation's teaching force is encountering an increasing number of children from immigrant families—children who speak little or no English on arrival at school and whose families may be unfamiliar with the demands of American schooling—the challenge is even greater. The U.S. teaching force is not well equipped to help these children and those who speak vernacular **dialects**[*] of English adjust to school, learn effectively and joyfully, and achieve academic success. Too few teachers share or know about their students' cultural and linguistic backgrounds or understand the challenges inherent in learning to speak and read Standard English. We argue in this paper that

[*]Words with underlining and bold are defined in a glossary, p. 44.

teachers lack this knowledge because they have not had the professional preparation they need.

The challenges of preparing teachers to work with immigrant and language minority children have been addressed previously. A book by Josué González and Linda Darling-Hammond (1997), *New Concepts for New Challenges: Professional Development for Teachers of Immigrant Youth,* provides an excellent discussion of professional development models that have been shown to work and the kinds of adaptations teachers of immigrant youth need to make. But the book deals only in passing with issues of language and literacy.

These issues have been brought to the foreground by changes in educational policy and practice over the past decade. Society has raised by quite a few notches the educational bar that all children in the United States, including newcomers, must clear in order to complete school successfully and, ultimately, to survive in the economic and social world of the 21st century. The adoption of Goals 2000 (1994) has raised curricular standards to levels that are more consistent with those in other societies. We have also adopted a system of benchmark assessments to evaluate the progress schools and students are making toward meeting those goals. In many states, policymakers have become impatient with the apparent failure of schools to educate students adequately at each level. They have ended the practice of "social promotion" whereby students are passed to the next grade each year whether or not they have met academic expectations. Policymakers in more than two dozen states have adopted high school proficiency examinations—tests of mathematics and English language and literacy—with high school diplomas at stake. Finally, there are signs that categories such as race and ethnicity, language background, and gender will no longer be considered in admissions decisions in higher education or in hiring. The assumption is that everyone will be judged strictly on their own merits and in comparison to universally applied norms. For university entrance, this means scoring at an acceptable level on standardized tests. For advancement in the university, it means passing writing proficiency assessments. Increasingly in the workplace, it means being a competent user of Standard English and being fully literate (Murnane & Levy, 1996).

These policies place tremendous pressure on children to become skilled users of language in school in order to achieve the levels of language and literacy competence required to pass through the gateways to high school graduation, college admission, and a good job. As it stands now, language minority students are not faring well under this pressure—but then, many other students are not doing so well either. Does this mean that the new standards and assessments are unreasonable? Are students not motivated or smart enough to handle higher levels of instruction? What do teachers need to know and be able to do in order to support their students' success? Do teachers lack the knowledge and skills necessary to help students? We will argue in this paper that teachers need a thorough understanding of how language figures in education, and for that reason they must receive systematic and intensive preparation in what we will call *educational linguistics.* A thorough grounding in educational linguistics would support teachers' undertakings overall, and in particular their capacity to teach literacy skills (see Snow, Burns, & Griffin, 1998) and to work with English language learners (see August & Hakuta, 1997). If approached coherently, such preparation would also, we contend, cover many of the items on that long list of desired teacher competencies compiled from state certification standards, relating as it would to skills in assessing children, in individualizing instruction, and in respecting diversity.

We begin here by presenting a rationale for current and prospective teachers to know more about language. We then turn to a brief specification of the sorts of knowledge that teachers need. This section first discusses requisite knowledge about oral language, then oral language used in formal and academic contexts, then written language. The final section of this chapter suggests courses that teacher preparation programs might offer to teacher candidates to cover the competencies required. This course list might also be seen as specifying aspects of an integrated, in-depth professional development program for in-service teachers. We use the course list, though, more to specify the range and types of information needed than as a prescription for teacher education programs, each of which will need to grapple with the mechanisms and formats for making the necessary information available.

# Why Do Teachers Need to Know More About Language?

We distinguish five functions for which prospective educators need to know more about language than they may be learning in teacher education programs:

- teacher as communicator
- teacher as educator
- teacher as evaluator
- teacher as educated human being
- teacher as agent of socialization

## Teacher as Communicator

Clearly, communication with students is essential to effective teaching. To communicate successfully, teachers must know how to structure their own language output for maximum clarity. They must also have strategies for understanding what students are saying, because understanding student talk is key to analysis of what students know, how they understand, and what teaching strategies would be useful. In a society that is experiencing increasingly diverse classrooms, teachers are increasingly likely to encounter students with whom they share neither a first language or dialect nor a native culture. An understanding of linguistics can help teachers see that the discourse patterns they value are aspects of their own cultures and backgrounds; they are neither universal nor inherently more valid than other possible patterns. Without such an understanding, teachers sometimes assume that there is something wrong with students whose ways of using language are not what they expect. Geneva Smitherman (1977) relates a poignant example of how teachers who do not recognize the validity of other ways of speaking can undermine their students' confidence in their own communicative abilities:

> Student (excitedly): Miz Jones, you remember that show you tole us about? Well, me and my momma 'nem—
>
> Teacher (interrupting with a "warm" smile): Bernadette, start again. I'm sorry, but I can't understand you.

Student (confused): Well, it was that show, me and my momma—

Teacher (interrupting again, still with that "warm" smile): Sorry, I still can't understand you.

(Student, now silent, even more confused than ever, looks at floor, says nothing.)

Teacher: Now Bernadette, first of all, it's *Mrs.* Jones, not *Miz* Jones. And you know it was an *exhibit*, not a *show*. Now, haven't I explained to the class over and over again that you always put yourself last when you are talking about a group of people and yourself doing something? So, therefore, you should say what?

Student: My momma and me—

Teacher (exasperated): No! My mother and I. Now start again, this time right.

Student: Aw, that's okay, it wasn't nothin.

(Smitherman, 1977, pp. 217-218)

Studies of discourse patterns in American Indian (Philips, 1993), Native Hawaiian (Boggs, 1972), Puerto Rican (Zentella, 1997), and African American (Heath, 1983) homes and communities have shown that the speech patterns that children bring to school from their homes can be quite different from the ones that are valued at school. These speech patterns are nonetheless essential to functioning effectively in their home communities. Acquiring the academic discourse patterns of school is an important part of the educational development of all students, but it is neither necessary nor desirable to promote it at the expense of the language patterns children already have. In fact, Mrs. Jones' pedagogical approach to language development is more likely to sour children like Bernadette to the whole experience of schooling than it is to instruct them.

In as diverse a society as ours, teachers must be prepared to work with children from many different cultural, social, and linguistic backgrounds. Many schools serve students who are learning English as a second language. Understanding the course of second language acquisition, including such matters as the sorts of mistakes English language learners are likely to make and how much progress can be expected in a unit of time, helps teachers communicate with these students more effectively. Even advanced speakers of English as a second language may use conversational patterns or narrative organization that differ from those of the mainstream. Understanding how their language use might differ from that of native European American English speakers is crucial for effective teaching. In their function as **interlocutor,** teachers need to know something about educational linguistics.

## Teacher as Educator

Teachers are responsible for selecting educational materials and activities at the right level and of the right type for all of the children in their classes. This requires that they have the expertise to assess student accomplishments and the capacity to distinguish between imperfect knowledge of English and cognitive obstacles to learning. In order to teach effectively, teachers need to know which language problems will resolve themselves with time and which need attention and intervention. In other words, they need to know a great deal about language development.

Language is a vital developmental domain throughout the years of schooling, whatever the child's linguistic, cultural, or social background. Textbooks on child development often claim that by age five or six children have already mastered the grammar of their native language and that although they expand their vocabularies in school and add literacy skills, for the most part children have acquired language before they go to school. Such a characterization of language development is far from accurate. All children have a long way to go developmentally before they can function as mature members of their speech communities (Hoyle & Adger, 1998). As they progress through the grades, children will acquire grammatical structures and strategies for the more sophisticated and precise ways of using language that are associated with maturity, formal language use, and the discussion of challenging topics.

Teachers play a critical role in supporting language development. Beyond teaching children to read and write in school, they can help children learn and use aspects of language associated with the academic discourse of the various school subjects. They can help them become more aware of how language functions in various modes of communication across the curriculum. They need to understand how language works well enough to select materials that will help expand their students' linguistic horizons and to plan instructional activities that give students opportunities to use the new forms and modes of expression to which they are being exposed. Teachers need to understand how to design the classroom language environment so as to optimize language and literacy learning and to avoid linguistic obstacles to content area learning. A basic knowledge of educational linguistics is prerequisite to promoting language development with the full array of students in today's classrooms.

## Teacher as Evaluator

Teachers' judgments can have enormous consequences for children's lives, from the daily judgments and responses that affect students' sense of themselves as learners to the more weighty decisions about reading group placement, promotion to the next grade, or referral for special education evaluation. American school culture is greatly concerned with individual differences in learning ability, and judgments about ability are often based on teacher evaluations of children's language. American educators take seriously the idea that people differ in abilities and aptitudes, and they believe that such differences require different treatment in school.[1] A lot of attention is given to sorting children by ability as early as possible. Children entering kindergarten are given readiness tests to determine which of them meet the developmental expectations of school and which do not. Some schools have developmental or junior kindergartens for children who are judged not quite ready for school from their performance on these readiness tests. In many kindergartens, children are grouped for instruction according to the notion of ability on the basis of such tests. If they are not grouped in this way in kindergarten, they certainly are by first grade (Michaels, 1981). Thus, well before children have had a chance to find out what school is about, they can be declared to be fast, middling, or slow learners (Oakes, 1985).

Such grouping is pernicious if it sorts children globally into differentiated groups. Once sorted this way, children typically receive substantially different instructional treatment and materials, reinforcing any initial differences among them in speed of learning and eagerness to learn. Later on, students who have been in classes for academically talented children behave like gifted and talented children: They are bright, verbal, and enthusiastic about school. Those who have been in lower groups behave precisely as one would expect low-ability students to behave: They are poorly motivated, low achieving, and less enthusiastic about school than they should be.

We do not mean to suggest here that children should never be sorted for any purpose. It is very effective for teachers to form small groups of children who need more time with particular instructional foci (e.g., **digraphs** or vocabulary enrichment or long vowel spellings). It can also be helpful to group children who read at a similar level so they can discuss their books with one another. But the key to such grouping is that it be targeted (i.e., used for a particular instructional purpose), flexible (i.e., as soon as individual children have acquired the targeted skill they leave that group), and objective (i.e., based on well-specified criteria directly related to the instructional target, not on global measures of readiness).

A serious worry about global tracking decisions is the questionable validity of the original assessments on which these placement decisions are made. Judgments of children's language and social behaviors weigh heavily in these assessments (Oller, 1992). Guided by a readiness checklist, kindergarten and first-grade teachers answer questions like the following about the children in their classes: Do they know their first and last name? Can they follow simple instructions? Can they ask questions? Can they answer them? Do they know the names of the colors in their crayon boxes? Can they produce short narratives? Do they know their mother's name?[2] Can they count to 10? The assumption is that all children at age 5 or 6 should have the specific abilities that are assessed, and anyone who does not is not ready for school. In reality, such abilities and skills are hardly universal nor are they indicative of learning ability. There are rather great differences across cultures in the kinds of linguistic accomplishments believed to be appropriate for children at any age. The kinds of skills that children bring from home reflect those differences in belief. In some cultures, for example, children are encouraged to listen rather than to ask questions of adults. Only rude and poorly reared children would chatter away in the presence of an authority figure like the teacher. When children do not perform as expected on a test, it does not necessarily mean that they are lacking in ability—particularly if they do not know the language in which the questions were asked. Given the diversity in our society, it is imperative to recognize that young children may differ considerably in their inventory of skills and abilities, and these differences should not be treated as reflecting deficiencies in ability.

To make valid judgments about students' abilities, teachers also need to understand the different sources of variation in language use—whether a particular pattern signals membership in a language community that speaks a vernacular variety of English, normal progress for a second language learner of English, normal deviations from the adult standard that are associated with earlier stages of development, or developmental delay or disorder. The overrepresentation of African American, Native American, and Latino children in special education placements suggests that normal language features associated with a vernacular variety of English or with learning English as a second language are often misinterpreted as an indication of developmental delay (Ortiz, 1992). The high percentage of special education referrals for English language learners and vernacular dialect speakers may simply reflect teachers' strategies for getting these children extra help, often from a speech-language pathologist who is relatively well trained in language development issues. But if teachers knew more about language, they could institute instructional processes in the classroom to address these children's needs.

Considering the potential harm of misconstruing children's language use, investing in educational linguistic training about the course of language development and about language variety seems a wise use of teacher preparation resources.

## Teacher as Educated Human Being

Teachers need to have access to basic information about language for the same reasons that any educated member of society should know something about language. Understanding the basics of how one's own language works contributes to proficient reading and writing. Recognizing the difference between nouns and verbs, consonants and vowels, or oral and literate forms is as basic for the liberally educated human being as is knowledge about addition and subtraction, nutrition, or the solar system. Students educated in the United States should also know something about differences between the structure of English and that of other languages just as surely as they should know about the tripartite organization of the U.S. government. It used to be the case that English grammar was taught to students beginning in about the fifth grade and continuing through eighth grade in what was then called grammar school. Such instruction was largely discontinued in the 1960s, except in Catholic schools. At least one foreign language would often also be included in the core curriculum. Not only are such subjects no longer required, in some places they are not taught at all. For some time now we have had teachers who had little exposure to the study of grammar when they were students.

Teachers who have not had the opportunity to study the structure of English or to learn another language understandably do not feel very confident talking about language. English is the language of society, it is the language most teachers use exclusively in their teaching, and it is the language that many teachers teach about to some extent. But how much do they know about it? Do they know its history? Do they know what languages are related to it? Do they know how it has changed over time, especially since the advent of the printing press? Do they know why there are so many peculiar spellings in English? Do they know how regional dialects develop? Teachers have practical, professional reasons to know these things, but we suggest that the attention to grammar and rhetoric that was characteristic of the lower level of a classical education was neither premature nor exaggerated. All of us should understand such matters, and we will not learn them unless teachers understand them first.

Throughout the United States, there is a real need for research-based knowledge about language teaching, language learning, and how language functions in education. We also need educational leadership to ensure that this knowledge is widely shared. Several recent events involved public discussions, with participation by teachers and other educators, that were alarmingly uninformed and uninsightful about language issues. These events include the passage of Proposition 227 in California in 1998 and subsequent attempts in other states to limit or eliminate bilingual education. Discussion of Proposition 227 revealed a dismaying lack of understanding about the facts of second language learning and the nature of bilingual education. Similarly, the Ebonics controversy that resulted from the Oakland School District's decision in 1996 to treat African American Vernacular English as a first language for many students raised issues that most people were ill-prepared to discuss in an informed way. Finally, the willingness of school districts and parent groups to embrace inappropriate methods for teaching reading in response to low performance on reading tests, to abandon theoretically sound methods for teaching English in the face of disappointing language achievement scores, and to adopt unproven approaches to foreign language teaching reminds us that too few people know enough of the basics about language and literacy to engage in reasonable discussion and to make informed decisions about such matters. Ideally teachers would be raising the level of such discussions by referring to research-based interventions.

## Teacher as Agent of Socialization

Teachers play a unique role as agents of socialization—the process by which individuals learn the everyday practices, the system of values and beliefs, and the means and manners of communication in their cultural communities. Socialization begins in the home and continues at school. When the cultures of home and school match, the process is generally continuous: Building on what they have acquired at home from family members, children become socialized into the ways of thinking and behaving that characterize educated individuals. They learn to think critically about ideas, phenomena, and experiences, and they add the modes and structures of academic **discourse** to their language skills. But when there is a mismatch between the cultures of home and school, the process can be disrupted. We have discussed some ways in which mismatches between teachers' expectations of how children should behave communicatively and how they actually do behave can affect teachers' ability to understand children, assess their abilities, and teach them effectively. In fact, what teachers say and do can determine how successfully children make the crucial transition from home to school. It can determine whether children move successfully into the world of the school and larger society as fully participating members or get shunted onto sidetracks that distance them from family, society, and the world of learning.

For many children, teachers are the first contact with the culture of the social world outside of the home. From associations with family members, children have acquired a sense of who they are, what they can do, what they should value, how they should relate to the world around them, and how they should communicate. These understandings are cultural—they differ from group to group and even within groups. Children of immigrants and native-born American children from non-majority backgrounds may encounter a stark disjunction between their cultural understandings and those of the school. For example, Mexican children generally have a sure sense of self within the world of the home. The center of this universe is not the individual but the family itself. Each member is responsible for maintaining, supporting, and strengthening the family; its needs come before the needs of any individual (Valdés, 1996). For Pueblo Indian children, the central unit is the community, and its needs and requirements take precedence over those of the individual (Popovi Da, 1969).[3]

When children from these cultures begin school, they encounter a culture that has a very different focus, one that emphasizes the primacy of the individual and considers family, group, and community needs subsidiary to individual needs. They soon discover that the school culture takes precedence over the home culture. Administrators and teachers do not accept as excuses for school absence the need to care for younger siblings when the mother is sick or to participate in a religious ritual in the community. Children learn that at school, work and progress are regarded as individual endeavors, and they are rewarded for the ability to work independently, without help and support from others.

In the area of language and communication, children who enter school with no English are expected to learn the school's language of instruction as quickly as possible, often with minimal help. Children discover very quickly that the only way they can have access to the social or academic world of school is by learning the language spoken there. The messages that may be conveyed to children and their parents are that the home language has no value or role in school if it is not English, and that parents who want to help their children learn English should switch to English for communication at home. For parents who know and speak English, this is not difficult (though it may be undesirable); for parents who do not know English well or at all, it is tantamount to telling them they have nothing to contribute to the education of their children.[4]

The process of socialization into the culture of the school need not be detrimental either to the child or to the family, even when there are substantial differences between the cultures of home and school. When teachers realize just how traumatic the assimilation process can be for immigrant and native-born children from non-majority backgrounds, given the adjustments and accommodations they must make as they move from the world of the home to the one at school, they can ease the process considerably. If teachers respect their students' home languages and cultures and understand the crucial role they play in the lives of the children and their families, they can help children make the necessary transitions in ways that do not undercut the role that parents and families must continue to play in their education and development.[5]

## What Should Classroom Teachers Know About Language?

In this section, we outline a set of questions that the average classroom teacher should be able to answer, and we identify topics that teachers and other educators should have knowledge of. We focus first on oral language, then on written language. These questions and topics are not arcane or highly technical. We are certainly not proposing that all educators need to understand Universal Grammar, Government and Binding Theory, Minimalist **Phonology,** or other topics of interest to the professional linguist. Rather, we are identifying issues of language use in daily life, issues that require only a basic understanding of the descriptive work that linguists engage in and the concepts that they use. Decisions about how to segment the information we call for—that is, how to distribute it over preservice courses and inservice learning—and how to ensure that it will be acquired go well beyond our brief. We simply provide a (no doubt incomplete) listing of issues and a brief justification for the relevance to classroom practice of each, in the hope that those with greater expertise in teacher education can think about how to make this knowledge available to classroom practitioners.

Attention to educational linguistics might be assumed to be of particular importance to the educator specialized in dealing with language learners—the bilingual or English as a second language (ESL) teacher. We certainly agree that prospective ESL and bilingual teachers would benefit from intensive and coherent preparation in educational linguistics. But we contend that such preparation is equally important for all classroom practitioners and, indeed, for administrators and educational researchers—though of course the specifics of more advanced preparation will vary for these groups. Expertise on language issues related to teaching and learning is important for all educators, increasingly so as the percentage of English language learners and speakers of vernacular dialects increases among American students.

## Oral Language

We begin by attending to oral language because in their native language (and often in a second language), children develop oral proficiency first. Oral language functions as a foundation for literacy and as the means of learning in school and out. However, despite its importance for learning, many teachers know much less about oral language than they need to know.

### What are the basic units of language?

Teachers need to know that spoken language is composed of units of different sizes: sounds (called **phonemes** if they function to signal different meanings in the language), **morphemes** (sequences of sounds that form the smallest units of meaning in a language), words (consisting of one or more morphemes), phrases (one or more words), sentences, and discourses. Crucial to an understanding of how language works is the idea of *arbitrariness*. Sequences of sounds have no meaning by themselves; it is only by convention that meanings are attached to sound. In another language, a sequence of sounds that is meaningful in English may mean nothing at all or something quite different.

Furthermore, each language has an inventory of phonemes that may differ from that of other languages. Phonemes can be identified by virtue of whether a change in sound makes a difference in meaning. For example, in English, *ban* and *van* constitute two different words, which show that [b] and [v] are different phonemes. Similarly, *hit* and *heat* are two different words, showing that the short vowel sound [I] of *hit* is different from the long vowel sound [i] of *heat*. In Spanish, however, the differences between [b] and [v] and between [I] and [i] do not make a difference in meaning. Native Spanish speakers may be influenced by the phonemic inventory of Spanish when they are speaking English. They might say *very good* or *bery good* to mean the same thing. Similarly, *it is little* and *eet eez leetle* have the same meaning. Dialects of English show different phonemic patterns as well. In southern U.S. varieties, for example, the vowels in *pin* and *pen* sound the same, but in northern varieties they sound different. It is clear that such contrasting phonemic patterns across languages and dialects can have an impact on what words children understand, how they pronounce them, and also how they might be inclined to spell them.

The morpheme is the smallest unit of language that expresses a distinct meaning. A morpheme can be an independent or free unit, like *jump, dog,* or *happy,* or it can be a prefix or suffix attached to another morpheme to modify its meaning, such as *−ed* or *−ing* for verbs (*jumped, jumping*), plural *−s* or possessive *−s* for nouns (*dogs, dog's*), or *−ly* or *−ness* added to adjectives to turn them into adverbs or nouns (*happily, happiness*). In other words, *jumped* is a single word that contains two morphemes, *jump* and *−ed*. Units like *-ed* or *−ly* are called bound morphemes because they do not occur alone. The relevance of bound morphemes to teachers' understanding emerges most strongly in the domain of spelling, discussed below. But it is worth noting here that English, reflecting its origin as a Germanic language, features many irregular forms (see Pinker, 1999) that can cause problems. Children may produce ungrammatical forms using regular morpheme combinations, such as past tense *bringed* and plural *mans*. And just as it is informative to study contrasts in phoneme patterns across dialects, teachers should also be aware of dialect variation in morpheme combinations. For example, in African American Vernacular English, the plural form of *man* can be *mens*.

Teachers need to understand that grammatical units such as bound and free morphemes, words, phrases, and clauses operate quite differently across languages. The **locative** meanings expressed by prepositions such as *in, on,* and *between* in English are expressed by noun endings (bound morphemes) in Hungarian, but they are often incorporated into the structure of the verb in Korean. In Chinese, plurality and past tense are typically expressed by separate words such as *several* and *already* rather than bound morphemes (*-s* and *−ed*), but these words may be omitted if these meanings are obvious in context. The native Chinese speaker who treats plurals and past tenses as optional rather than obligatory in English is reflecting the rules of Chinese. Of course such a learner needs to learn how to produce grammatical English sentences. But understanding the variety of structures that different languages and dialects use to show meaning, including grammatical meaning such as plurality or past tense, can help teachers see the logic behind the errors of their students who are learning English. When 2-year-olds produce forms like *I swinged already,* we consider it charming; we need to see that the errors of older second language speakers reflect the same level of creativity.

Finally, teachers need knowledge about the larger units of language use—sentence and discourse structure—that are fundamental to understanding the unique features of academic language. We have pointed out that teachers' expectations for students' participation in classroom talk may be based on the teachers' own cultural patterns. Such simple rhetorical tasks as responding to questions require making a hypothesis about why the question is being asked and how it fits into a set of social relationships that may be specific to a culture. *Can you open the door?* might be a question about physical strength or psychological willingness, or it might be a request. If a child gives a puzzling response to a question, the teacher who knows something about cross-linguistic differences in the rules for asking questions and making requests might well be able to analyze its source. It is critical that interpretations of language use as reflecting politeness, intelligence, or other characteristics of the student be informed by this understanding of language differences.

Trouble can occur at the discourse level when students do not understand teachers' expectations about academic discourse patterns that the teachers themselves learned in school. For example, in the interactive structure typical of direct instruction, the teacher initiates an interaction, often by asking a question; a student responds; then the teacher evaluates the response. Asking a question in the response slot can risk teacher censure (Zuengler & Cole, 2000). It is unlikely that teachers are aware of their expectations for students' participation in classroom discourse. Implicit norms for language use are part of what it means to know a language well. When teachers have explicit knowledge of rhetorical structures, they have the tools for helping children understand the expectations associated with school English.

## What's regular and what isn't? How do forms relate to each other?

By virtue of being proficient English speakers and effortless readers, most adults take for granted language irregularities that can be enormously puzzling to younger and less fluent learners. Is there any difference between *dived* and *dove*? Can one similarly say both *weaved* and *wove*? Why do we say *embarrassment, shyness, likeliness,* and *likelihood,* not *embarrassness* or *embarrasshood, shyment, shyhood,* or *likeliment*? Such questions may seem odd, but they arise naturally during children's language development. Answers lie in principles of word formation rooted in the history of English.

An important part of acquiring a vocabulary suitable for academic contexts is learning how to parse newly encountered words into their component parts, rather than simply treating complex words as long words. In many cases, the context in which a word is used and the recognition of familiar morphemes assist in interpreting and remembering words. There are probably thousands of words that most people learn in context without help, for example, *disinherit, pre-established,* and *decaffeinated.* The key here is that there are regular patterns for how word parts (morphemes) can be combined into longer words.

Teachers should be aware of the principles of word formation in English because such knowledge can aid their students in vocabulary acquisition. They should be aware, for example, of such patterns as the *d/s* alternation in pairs of related words like *evade* and *evasive, conclude* and *conclusive.* When they know this principle, students can learn two new words at once. Teachers should be aware of certain accent-placement regularities involving the suffixes written *-y* and *—ic,* so that they can help students learn groups of words together: for example, *SYNonym, syNONymy, synoNYMic; PHOtograph, phoTOGraphy, photoGRAPHic; ANalog, aNALogy, anaLOGic,* and so on. A mastery of the connections between the patterns of word formation and the rhythms of English speech should equip teachers to point out such patterns in academic language and enhance students' vocabulary growth.

Spanish-speaking children can be taught to use correlated morphological structures in Spanish and English to understand sophisticated English lexical items and to expand their English vocabularies. Consider the advantages for Spanish speakers who discover that a Spanish noun that ends in *-idad* almost always has an English **cognate** that ends in -*ity* (*natividad* and *nativity, pomposidad* and *pomposity, curiosidad* and *curiosity*) or that nouns ending in -*idumbre* relate to nouns ending in -*itude* (*certidumbre* and *certitude, servidumbre* and *servitude*). If they already know the Spanish words, the parallel to English can be pointed out; if they do not know the word in either language, the parallel Spanish and English words can be taught together.

Students who come to English as native speakers of other **Indo-European languages** may find it helpful to be aware of the international vocabulary of science and technology (e.g., *photosynthesis* is *fotosíntesis* in Spanish, *fotosintez* in Russian; *computer* is *computador* or *computadora* in Spanish, *kompyuter* in Russian). This could involve learning basic correspondences, the notion of cognate and how to distinguish cognates from false cognates and loan words, enough about the history of English to be able to judge whether an English word is likely to have a cognate in the student's first language, and cross-linguistic comparisons. In order to teach these matters, teachers must understand them deeply and know how to support their students' explorations when the teacher does not know the other language involved.

## How is the **lexicon** acquired and structured?

Almost every classroom teacher recognizes the need to teach vocabulary (the lexicon), and most teachers do so. Usually, technical or unusual words used in texts are targeted for instruction. Definitions for each one are solicited from the students or are supplied by the teacher before the text is read in interactions along these lines:

> Teacher: *Digestion:* Who knows what *digestion* means?
>
> Student: I know, I know. When you eat.
>
> Teacher: That's right! When we eat, we digest our food. That's *digestion!*

Often, the definitions given are rather superficial and sometimes even misleading, as in this example. The definition offered here would work better for *ingestion* than for *digestion*. Presumably the text itself and the ensuing class discussion would clarify the meaning of *digestion,* but the initial instructional effort probably added little to the children's understanding. It takes many encounters with a word in meaningful contexts for students to acquire it (Beck, McKeown, & Omanson, 1987).

What does it mean to acquire a word? What do we know when we know a word? Knowing a word involves knowing something of its core meaning. In the case of *digestion,* the core meaning is the process by which the food one eats is converted into simpler forms that the body can use for energy. But few words are unidimensional in meaning or use, so knowing a word goes well beyond knowing a definition of it. Knowing a word requires also an understanding of how it relates to similar forms (e.g., *digestion, digest, ingest, digestive, indigestion*), how it can be used grammatically (i.e., its word class and the grammatical constructions it can be used in), and how it relates to other words and concepts (e.g., *food, nutrient, stomach, digestive juices, esophagus, intestines, digesting facts, Reader's Digest*). Vocabulary instruction could be more effective if teachers understood how words are learned in noninstructional contexts, through conversational interactions, and through encounters with written language. Knowing individual words more deeply is as important as knowing more words.

For children growing up in English-speaking families, rapid English vocabulary acquisition is the rule. According to George Miller (1976, 1987), between ages 1 and 17, children add 13 words per day to their growing vocabulary, adding up to around 80,000 words by the time they are 17. Very little of this is achieved with the help of teachers or dictionaries. Vocabulary acquisition happens most easily in context and related to topics that children care about. The teacher's responsibility lies mainly in setting up exposure to language in a vivid way and encouraging reading of material that children care about.

For second language learners, it is perhaps most valuable to stage exposure to new vocabulary items in related groups, since many words are more meaningful when they are understood in connection with other words related to the same general topic. (For an accessible discussion of how the mental lexicon is thought to be organized, see Aitchison, 1994; for a discussion of how bilinguals and monolinguals differ in their treatment of words, see Merriman & Kutlesic, 1993.) Thus, talk about *mothers* and *fathers* should include talk about *brothers* and *sisters*, *grandfathers* and *grandmothers*; talk about *buying* should include talk about *selling, paying, money,* and *getting change.* Some understanding of how translations can differ from one another in subtle aspects of meaning and use can aid in supporting the lexical acquisition of the second language learner.

## Are vernacular dialects different from "bad English" and, if so, how?

Given the diversity in social and cultural backgrounds of the students they serve, practitioners and researchers whose work or study focuses on teaching and learning in schools must have a solid grounding in sociolinguistics and in language behavior across cultures. Like other languages, English has dialects associated with geographical regions and social classes and distinguished by contrasts in their sound system, grammar, and lexicon. Standard dialects are considered more prestigious than vernacular dialects, but this contrast is a matter of social convention alone. Vernacular dialects are as regular as standard dialects and as useful. Facts about normal language variation are not widely known, as demonstrated by the misunderstandings about language, language behavior, and language learning revealed in the national response to the Oakland (CA) School Board's Ebonics proposal. The proposal amounted to a declaration that the language spoken in the homes of many of its African American students should be regarded as a language in its own right and should not be denigrated by teachers and administrators as slang, street talk, or bad English. It further declared its support of the school district's efforts to seek funds for the Standard English Proficiency Program, which uses children's home language to teach school English. This idea was certainly not radical, but the Ebonics story continued to be news for nearly 2 months. It was the focus of talk shows on radio and television. It was featured in front-page newspaper stories for nearly a month and even longer in editorial pages, political cartoons, and news magazines. The U.S. Senate held special hearings. The Oakland School Board's proposal was denounced, ripped apart, and ridiculed. Why was it controversial? This is how Lisa Delpit (1997) responded when asked, "What do you think about Ebonics? Are you for it or against it?"

> My answer must be neither. I can be neither for Ebonics nor against Ebonics any more than I can be for or against air. It exists. It is the language spoken by many of our African-American children. It is the language they heard as their mothers nursed them and changed their diapers and played peek-a-boo with them. It is the language through which they

first encountered love, nurturance and joy. On the other hand, most teachers of those African-American children who have been least well-served by educational systems believe that their students' life chances will be further hampered if they do not learn Standard English. In the stratified society in which we live, they are absolutely correct. (p. 6)

Schools must provide children who speak vernacular varieties of English the support they need to master the English required for academic development and for jobs when they have completed school. The process does not work when the language spoken by the children—the language of their families and primary communities—is disrespected in school. This is as true for a vernacular variety of English as it is for another language such as Navaho, Yup'ik, Cantonese, or Spanish. A recognition of how language figures in adults' perceptions of children and how adults relate to children through language is crucial to understanding what happens in schools and how children ultimately view schools and learning.

How do dialect differences affect language learning and literacy development? Even if practitioners have enough knowledge to prevent speakers of vernacular dialects from being misdiagnosed and misplaced in school programs, they need a good understanding about language variability in order to make educational decisions that ensure effective instruction. Knowledge of the natural course of language acquisition and of the capacity of the individual to maintain more than one dialect is crucial in making such choices.

## What is academic English?

Although there is a lot of discussion about the need for all children to develop the English language skills required for academic learning and development, few people can identify exactly what those skills consist of or distinguish them from general Standard English skills. To the extent that this matter is examined at all, observers have usually pointed to differences between written and spoken language. However, academic English entails a broad range of language proficiencies. We must ask what linguistic proficiencies are required for subject-matter learning. Is academic language proficiency just a matter of vocabulary learning, or is it more? Cummins (1981b, 1984) has described academic language as cognitively demanding, its most obvious feature being that it is relatively decontextualized. It relies on broad knowledge of words, **phraseology**, grammar, discourse structure, and pragmatic conventions for expression, understanding, and interpretation.

A recent study of prototype test items for a high school graduation examination for one of the 26 states that require students to pass an exam in order to receive a diploma revealed that whatever else is being assessed, competence in the register that we refer to as academic English is necessary to pass (Fillmore, 1999). The language used in this test is the language ordinarily used in textbooks and discussions about science, mathematics, literature, or social studies. To pass this test, students have to be able to do the following:

- Summarize texts, using linguistic cues to interpret and infer the writer's intentions and messages.
- Analyze texts, assessing the writer's use of language for rhetorical and aesthetic purposes and to express perspective and mood.
- Extract meaning from texts and relate it to other ideas and information.
- Evaluate evidence and arguments presented in texts and critique the logic of arguments made in them.
- Recognize and analyze textual conventions used in various genres for special effect to trigger background knowledge or for **perlocutionary effect.**
- Recognize ungrammatical and infelicitous usage in written language and make necessary corrections to grammar, punctuation, and capitalization.
- Use grammatical devices for combining sentences into concise and more effective new ones, and use various devices to combine sentences into coherent and cohesive texts.
- Compose and write an extended, reasoned text that is well developed and supported with evidence and details.
- Interpret word problems—recognizing that in such texts, ordinary words may have specialized meanings (e.g., that *share equally among them* means to divide a whole into equal parts).
- Extract precise information from a written text and devise an appropriate strategy for solving a problem based on information provided in the text.

The production and understanding of academic English are issues for English language learners and for native speakers of English alike. Few children arrive at school fully competent in the language required for text interpretation and for the kind of reasoned discourse we assume is a key to becoming an edu-cated person. Possible exceptions are the children of academics and other highly educated professionals who use this register even at home, read a lot to their children, and engage them in discussions about a wide range of topics. For the most part, however, academic English is learned at school from teach-ers and from textbooks. Written texts are a reliable source of academic English, but they serve as the basis for language development only with instructional help. Teachers provide the help that students need to acquire this register when they go beyond discussions of content to discussions of the lan-guage used in texts for rhetorical and aesthetic effect.

To provide such instructional support, teachers need to know something about how language figures in academic learning and recognize that all stu-dents require instructional support and attention to acquire the forms and structures associated with it. This is especially true for English language learn-ers. Often, explicit teaching of language structures and uses is the most effec-tive way to help learners. A focus on language is crucial, no matter what subject is being taught. Children must engage in classroom discussions of sub-ject matter that are more and more sophisticated in form and content. And teachers must know enough about language to discuss it and to support its development in their students. Academic language is learned through frequent exposure and practice over a long period of time—from the time children enter school to the time they leave it.

## Why has the acquisition of English by non-English-speaking children not been more universally successful?

It appears that non-English-speaking students may be having a harder and harder time learning English. Although it used to take them from 5 to 7 years to learn English to a high level (Cummins, 1981a; Klesmer, 1994), recent studies suggest it is now taking 7 to 10 years (Ramírez, Pasta, Yuen, Billings, & Ramey, 1991). There are students who begin school in kindergarten classified by their school district as limited English proficient (LEP) and who leave it as LEP students 13 years later.

Inadequacies in English lead to academic problems, of course, and many stu-dents drop out of school or are pushed out well before graduation (Olsen, Jaramillo, McCall-Perez, & White, 1999). Surprisingly, though, some of these students do rather well academically—well enough in math and science courses to be admitted to the University of California system, for example. But Robin Scarcella, who directs the English as a Second Language Program at the Irvine campus of the University of California, reports that in 1997, 60% of the freshmen who took the English composition competency test failed. Of this group, one third had major problems with English language skills that required enrollment in ESL classes designed to help them acquire academic English. Ninety-five percent of the 603 students enrolled in these ESL classes had lived in the United States for more than 8 years. On average, they had taken 1 year of specially designed English classes for nonnative English speakers in elementary or junior high school. Most of the students had earned honors in high school, ranking among the top 12% of their high school graduating classes; 65% of them had taken honors and Advanced Placement English courses. Nevertheless, their English writing indicated that they did not have a sure sense of how English works. Consequently, they had serious problems meeting the language demands of university-level work (Scarcella, in press). Why are their language and writing skills so poor?

The public, the press, and many educators have blamed bilingual education for the slow rate of English learning and poor outcomes of English language learners. But as the case cited above suggests, the problem is not limited to the approximately 30% of English language learners who have studied in bilingual programs; those in all-English instructional settings show similarly disappointing outcomes (Hakuta, 2001).

California, with its very high incidence of English language learners—currently 1.4 million, or 25% of the school population (California State Department of Education, 2001)[6] —was the first place that bilingual education was attacked as contributing to problems of students learning English. In 1998, California's voters passed Proposition 227, essentially banning bilingual education in that state. Many people who voted for this initiative believed that bilingual education made it possible for English language learners to avoid learning English (Fillmore, in press). However, several studies (e.g., Collier, 1992; Collier & Thomas, 1989; Ramírez et al., 1991) have found that students in well-designed bilingual programs master English more rapidly (5 to 7 years) than do students in English-only programs (7 to 10 years).

It is often assumed that students who do not learn English rapidly or well are mostly Spanish speakers whose everyday interactions, even in school, are with other Spanish speakers. These students do not thrive academically, we are told, because they are not motivated to learn English or to do the work that school requires. A close look at these students suggests that this assumption is not valid. Non-Spanish speakers are well represented among the group that does not learn English well, including many Asians who have been in English-only classes since the time they entered school. Furthermore, many of these Asian students no longer speak their first languages even at home with family members (Schmida, in press; Schmida & Chiang, 1999).

Whether or not English language learners manage to survive in school, few can learn English at the levels required for success in higher education or the workplace without well-designed instructional intervention, particularly if the only native English speakers they encounter in daily life are their teachers. But for many years, teachers who work with these students have been unclear about what instructional role they should play in second language learning. Over the past two decades, some teacher education programs and in-service workshops have suggested that there is no need for teachers to provide explicit instruction in English grammar, vocabulary, and so forth. Instead, teachers have been told by experts that they should speak to children in ways that help them understand and teach them subject matter using simplified English. They should use pictures, gestures, demonstrations and the like to allow children to acquire English naturally and automatically, and they should avoid indicating that they notice students' English language errors so that learners will not be self-conscious and immobilized in using the language. The message is this: Direct instruction can do nothing to change the course of language development, which is determined by internal language acquisition mechanisms that allow learners to sort things out eventually.

Are these approaches effective? Examining how children acquire English in a variety of settings, Fillmore (1982, 1991) found that certain conditions must be met if children are to be successful. They must interact directly and frequently with people who know the language well enough to reveal how it works and how it can be used. During interactions with English learners, expert speakers not only provide access to the language at an appropriate level, they also provide ample clues as to what the units in the language are and how they combine to communicate ideas, information, and intentions. Learners receive corrective feedback as they negotiate and clarify communicative intentions (Long, 1985; Pica, 1996). The acquisition process can go awry when the conditions for language learning are not met, especially when learners greatly outnumber people who know the language well enough to support acquisition, as in schools and classrooms with high populations of English language learners.

When there is no direct instruction in such situations, children can either make little progress learning English, or they can learn it from one another (Fillmore, 1992). The outcome is "Learnerese," an interlanguage pidgin (Schmida, 1996) that can deviate considerably from Standard English. Students who speak this variety, sometimes called "ESL Lifers," have settled into a variety of English that is fairly stable and that many of them speak fluently and with confidence. They are no longer language learners, because they are no longer working out the details of English. The following text, produced in an exchange between Schmida and a student she calls Ti-Sang, exemplifies Learnerese. Ti-Sang had said that she does not find it easy to communicate with her parents, because she can hardly speak Khmer, and they do not speak English. Asked about her cousins who had immigrated not long before from Cambodia, Ti-Sang responded,

> Hmm . . . they—they, like, speak Cambodian more because
> they more comfortable in it. They don't want to talk English
> sometime because—when they go to school they don't, like,
> really talking, right? But when at home they chatter-talk.
> 'Cause they kind of shy, you know, like, when the teacher call
> on them and they don't know the answer, sometime they
> know the answer but they shy to answer. If you ask them, ask
> them so quietly, they answer.

At age 12, Ti-Sang had been in English-only classes for 8 years, from the time she entered school.

We argue that the poor language outcomes for English language learners in California and elsewhere could have been avoided had teachers known enough about the conditions for successful second language learning to provide explicit instruction in English. Educators must know enough about language learning and language itself to evaluate the appropriateness of various methods, materials, and approaches for helping students make progress in learning English.

## Written Language

Written language is not merely oral language written down. To help their students acquire literacy, teachers need to know how written language contrasts with speech. Here we discuss questions about written language that teachers should be able to answer.

### Why is English spelling so complicated?

Since the first sound in *sure* and *sugar* is different from the first sound in *sun* and *soup*, why aren't these words spelled differently? Why don't we spell the /s/ sound in *electricity* with an *s*? Why are there so many peculiar spellings among highly frequent words like *have, said, might,* and *could*? How can *oo* spell three different vowel sounds, as in the vampire's favorite line that mosquitoes say when they sit down to dine, "Blood is good food!"?

These and other peculiarities of English spelling reflect two facts about English **orthography**:

- Unlike French, Spanish, Dutch, and many other languages, English has never had a language academy charged with regular review and reform of spelling to eliminate inconsistencies and reflect language change.
- English generally retains the spelling of morphological units, even when the rules of pronunciation mean that phonemes within these morphological units vary (e.g., *electric, electricity, electrician*).

These two forces have led to what is called a *deep orthography* for English—an orthography in which the match of sound and spelling is complex and dependent on many factors. This is not to say that English spelling is illogical, irrational, or impossible to teach. However, some insight into the forces that have generated English spelling patterns can help teachers teach more effectively and understand children's errors.

It is helpful to consider the wide array of writing systems that exist in the world's languages (see Daniels & Bright, 1996). Some languages, such as Chinese, represent morphemes or semantically meaningful units with their graphemic symbols. Others, such as the Japanese katakana system, represent syllables instead. Both of these systems (morphemic and syllabic) have the advantage of being rather easy for young children, since morphemes and syllables are psychologically more accessible units than phonemes, which are simply sounds and often difficult to segment. In alphabetic writing systems, letters typically represent phonemes. Representing sounds alphabetically is fairly straightforward in languages that have experienced spelling reform, such as Spanish, and those that have adopted writing rather recently, such as Hmong. English, though, like Danish and German to some extent, often ignores phoneme identity to preserve the spelling identity of morphemes. For example, in English the spelling *s* is used for plural morphemes whether they are pronounced /s/ or /z/—even though in other contexts, such as at the beginning of words, the /s/ and /z/ sounds are spelled distinctively. Compare the spelling and pronunciation of *dogs* and *cats* to that of *zoo* and *Sue*. Similarly, the root form *electric* is retained even in forms where the final c represents quite a different sound from the /k/ in *electric*, including the /s/ of *electricity* and the /š/ of *electrician*.

The fact that the spelling *electric* is retained in all related word forms actually makes reading and inferring word meanings easier. Similarly, there is an advantage to writing *t* in both *complete* and *completion* and in both *activity* and *action*, even though the sounds that it stands for vary. The spelling makes it easier to see that the two words are morphologically related. For the same reason, it is probably good that we use the same letter for the three different vowel sounds between *p* and *t* in the words *compete*, *competitive*, and *competition*.

Other aspects of English spelling are less helpful. For example, *gh* in words like *night*, *through*, and *thought* is left over from a sound that has long since disappeared from English. Such spellings signal etymological relationships with words in other Germanic languages. English also tends to retain spellings that indicate the source of borrowed words, e.g., *ph* for /f/ and *y* for /ai/ in Greek origin words (*phone*, *hypothesis*). Such patterns increase the information available to the reader, but they do exacerbate the problems of decoding and spelling.

Some understanding of such complexities in English orthography can help teachers take sensible approaches to teaching the alphabetic principle in English. Teachers should know about the sound system of English and the history of language contact and development that has affected our writing system, because these factors can make simplistic phonics approaches inadvisable in teaching English reading.

Errors in spelling English can result from writers' inclination to write what they hear. Second language speakers' spelling errors can reflect inadequate exposure to written English forms, lack of adequate instruction in the nature of the English orthographic system, or transfer of general spelling strategies from another language. Some languages with alphabetic systems, such as Arabic or Tigrinya, are basically syllabic in their written representation: They focus on spelling the consonants in syllables, designating the vowels sketchily or omitting them entirely. Some languages, such as Spanish, with spelling systems that are quite phonemic, adjust spellings to reflect pronunciation even in closely related words (compare, for example, the related forms *saco* and *saqúe*). Other languages represent historical facts in their spelling, retaining information about the source language of borrowed lexical items. Japanese is one of these. Knowing how the orthographies of different languages are organized can help teachers figure out what sorts of spelling rules learners are likely to find easy or hard, what first language skills learners can rely on, and why students make certain types of errors. Understanding that there can be substantial differences in how symbols are used to represent sounds in different languages will help teachers be more effective in working with students who have had some prior literacy instruction in their native languages—students who have learned to read in Spanish, Vietnamese, French, and so forth, before entering an English reading program. The relationship between sounds and symbols can be relatively simple and straightforward in one language and much more complex in another.

## Why do some children have more trouble than others in developing early reading skills?

The problems beginning readers encounter can seem overwhelming and incomprehensible to a teacher who has not had a chance to learn about the complexities of the reading process. Knowledge about language is crucial in helping teachers do a better job of teaching initial reading (Snow et al., 1998).

Effective reading instruction requires integrating attention to the system of phoneme/**grapheme** mappings with attention to meaning. Children may encounter difficulties because they do not understand the basic principle of alphabetic writing—that letters represent sounds—or because they cannot segment the sounds reliably, or because they don't know the words they are expected to be reading. Second language learners are particularly likely to have difficulty producing, remembering, and distinguishing the target phonemes and to lack the knowledge of pronunciation that would help them in decoding (Ruddell & Unrau, 1997).

An additional problem arises when teachers who do not understand the complexities of English reading give tutors or teacher aides the responsibility for teaching reading to children who need the most help. These individuals are far less qualified to teach reading than are teachers. Even more problematic, teachers may assign English language learners to peer tutors for help with reading on the grounds that children can communicate more effectively with other children than with adults. But it takes a solid understanding of language to teach reading effectively, especially to children who are having the greatest difficulty grasping the abstract and complex relationships between sound and print, and who may be unfamiliar with the ideas the print is trying to convey. Teachers cannot make the learning of reading in English effortless, but they should be clearly aware of where and why the difficulties exist.

## Why do students have trouble with structuring narrative and expository writing?

All students need to learn the rhetorical structures associated with story-telling and expository writing in English. However, some students bring to this task culturally based text structures that contrast with those expected at school. The emphasis in mainstream English stories is on getting the order of events correct and clear. This emphasis can seem so obviously right to a monolingual speaker of English that the narrative of the Latino child, which emphasizes personal relationships more than plot, or of the Japanese child, who may provide very terse stories rather than recounting all of the events, may be dismissed as incomprehensible (McCabe, 1995). Different cultures focus on different aspects of an episode. Understanding a child's story requires knowing what information the child considers most important; such knowledge can help teachers guide students in acquiring the story structure valued at school.

Similarly with expository writing, argument structures vary considerably across cultures. There is no best way to make a point: Different ways make sense in different cultures. The topic sentences, paragraphs, and compare-and-contrast essays that are staples of English prose may be more difficult to learn for students whose language experience includes other structures. Understanding the absence of some of these concepts in literacy traditions associated with other languages or the extremely differing conceptions of how any of them should be structured can prevent teachers from mistakenly attributing language or cognitive disorders to students who have transferred a native language rhetorical style to English.

## How should one judge the quality and correctness of a piece of writing?

Educators must have a solid enough knowledge of grammar to support children's writing development. They need to make use of information about grammatical structure to pinpoint the problems many students have in writing or in interpreting text, and they need to be able teach students about language structure that they can draw on in their writing.

Partly because teachers feel insecure about their own knowledge of grammar, and partly because teachers of writing are sometimes reluctant to correct students' writing, students may not get the kind of informative feedback they must have in order to become more effective writers. The problem is particularly acute for learners of English as a second language. We have discussed above the problems encountered by many students learning English at the Irvine campus of the University of California. Some of these students reported that they had not previously received any of the explicit help with English or writing that they were getting at the university. Few had any idea that they could not write in grammatically or stylistically appropriate English. It was shocking for those who had been honor students to find themselves in remedial English courses, learning some of the fundamentals of English grammar and composition.

This state of affairs is not confined to UC Irvine or to students learning English. Across the 22 campuses of the California State University System, all entering freshmen take a placement test in English and math. The failure rate on the English Placement Test across the campuses in 1998 was 47%; at one campus, it was 80% (California State University, 2000). Students who fail the test are required to take and pass remedial English courses that focus on acquiring the language and literacy skills required for university-level work.

To provide the kind of feedback that students need to polish their writing, teachers need to understand English structure, discuss structural features of written language with their students, and explicitly teach them how to write effectively.

## What makes a sentence or a text easy or difficult to understand?

Many educators associate simple, short sentences with ease in understanding and interpretation. For that reason, texts that are prepared and selected for English language learners and other students who have trouble reading are often composed of short, choppy sentences. The result is unnatural, incoherent text conveying less substance than regular texts. One teacher described the materials being used with fourth-grade ESL students as "first grade materials, very basic—it isn't see Spot run, but it's close" (Gebhard, 2000). Do greatly simplified materials help or hurt comprehension? Examination of texts that had been modified according to the readability formulas used by textbook publishers found that such texts are often more difficult to interpret (Davison & Kantor, 1982). These texts require the reader to infer how sentences relate to each other, because to make sentences short, words and grammatical structures that show rhetorical or narrative connections between ideas are often eliminated.

The following text exemplifies the modifications found in simplified textbooks for low-achieving and ESL students:

> Using limestone to make other things
>
> We can use limestone to make other useful materials. To do this we have to use chemical reactions.
>
> Limestone is a rock that is made mostly from calcium carbonate.

If you heat limestone strongly you produce a gas called car-
bon dioxide. The substance left behind is called calcium
oxide.

Calcium oxide is also called quicklime. (Milner, Martin, &
Evans, 1998, p. 174)

Text simplification is achieved by restricting the number of words used. This
text contains just 61 words distributed among 7 sentences, including the
heading. The average number of words per sentence for this text is 8.7. When
texts are prepared with tight constraints on length, that becomes a greater
concern than any other criteria that might guide the preparation of such a
text, such as informativeness, relevance, coherence, naturalness, and grace. The
end result is that such texts are not only uninspiring and insulting to the
reader, but often less readable than the normal texts for that grade level.

Because simplified texts are often unnatural, they cannot serve as exemplars
of written academic English. Well-written texts with grade-level appropriate
language can give students access to the register of English that is used in
academic writing. With teachers' help, students can use these texts to learn
the vocabulary, grammatical structures, phraseology, and rhetorical devices
that are associated with that register. Learning to understand and produce
academic English is a goal not only for English language learners but for
native speakers of English too. But teachers must be able to call students'
attention to good examples of how language is used in text in order to support better student writing.

Teachers and school administrators play a nontrivial role in determining how
textbooks are written. Because textbook publishers can stay in business only
if states and school districts adopt their materials, they tend to be attuned to
what educators want. In the process of designing a series or an individual
textbook, publishers produce prototype materials that they market test on
school administrators who they hope will purchase the texts and on teachers
who they hope will select them. Educators need to develop a sure sense about
what is appropriate for students at different grade levels so that they can make
wise decisions in selecting and using text materials. To do that, they need to
know enough about language to assess the appropriateness of the language

used in texts, particularly for students who are learning English or who are having difficulty learning to read.

# Courses Teachers Need to Take

Although it would go beyond our brief to propose any specific curriculum for teacher education, we offer here a listing of possible courses or course components that together cover fundamental issues in the education of English language learners and other students for whom literacy and language learning in school contexts might be problematic.

## Language and Linguistics

This course would provide an introduction to linguistics motivated by the educational considerations we have mentioned—language structure, language in literacy development, language use in educational settings, the history of English, and the basics of linguistic analysis. We envision a language and linguistics course for educators that is different in focus from an introductory course for students of linguistics. Each area of linguistic study would be introduced by educational situations in which language is an issue. For example, the study of phonology could begin with an examination of interference problems that English language learners might have with the English sound system. It might include investigation of topics such as why speakers of Cantonese or Spanish have problems with consonant clusters at the ends of English words like *sixths*, which contains four consonants in a row: /sIkθs/.

## Language and Cultural Diversity

This course would focus on cultural contrasts in language use, particularly those likely to be encountered in teaching and learning. It would address such questions as what children learn when they acquire a language and culture, why some groups of children appear reluctant to participate in classroom discussions, and how differences in discourse styles can be accommodated in the classroom. This course would also examine different types of communication systems, including the language of deaf communities.

# Sociolinguistics for Educators in a Linguistically Diverse Society

A sociolinguistics course for educators would focus on language policies and politics that affect schools, including language attitudes in intergroup relations that affect students and language values. It would also address language contact, language shift and loss or isolation, and the role and the history of bilingualism in schools and society. Students would gain fundamental understandings about the nature of dialects and their connection to social identity.

## Language Development

This course would introduce issues in language development, with a special focus on academic language development in school-age children. It would address language development in native speakers of vernacular and standard English dialects, as well as in those who speak other languages. The course would address the role of literacy in the development of language skills and the acquisition of the structures and vocabulary required for literacy development.

## Second Language Learning and Teaching

Focusing on theoretical and practical knowledge about how second language acquisition proceeds and the factors that affect it, this course would compare second language learning to first language learning and examine the role of the primary language in second language learning. It would address second language instruction and subject-matter instruction in the language that students are acquiring. The course would also address the question of how proficient children must be in a second language before they can learn to read and write in that language.

## The Language of Academic Discourse

This course would focus on the language used in teaching and learning school subjects, especially the structure of academic discourse and how this register contrasts with that of informal communication. The course would show how language production and language understanding interact with content learning—science, social science, math, and so on—and how children's language development is promoted or not depending on how language is used in instructional activities.

### Text Analysis and Language Understanding in Educational Settings

A course like this would examine how language structures and style in written texts affect comprehensibility. It would guide teachers in deciding what aspects of text to target for instructional attention. A special focus of this course would be the needs of English language learners and vernacular dialect speakers in processing text.

# Conclusion

We have sketched here the reasons that educators need to know about language, the kinds of knowledge about language that they need, and an inventory of courses or course topics that would cover this crucial core of knowledge. This proposal may strike some readers as utopian. We acknowledge that we have formulated it without thinking about the structures and constraints of traditional teacher education programs. Nonetheless, we are energized by the current political situation surrounding debates about bilingual education and the rather frantic search for better methods of teaching reading. The substance of these debates gives striking testimony to the historical paucity of relevant expertise on language among those who are in the best position to improve public knowledge—educational practitioners (see, for example, Pressley, 1998; Snow et al., 1998).

It is clear that many of the challenges we face in education stem from the fact that ours is a diverse society. Students in our schools come from virtually every corner of the planet, and they bring to school diverse outlooks, languages, cultural beliefs and behaviors, and background experiences. Teachers in our schools have not always known what to do with the differences they encounter in their classrooms. As a society, we expect teachers to educate whoever shows up at the schoolhouse, to provide their students the language and literacy skills to survive in school and later on in jobs, to teach them all of the school subjects that they will need to know about as adults, and to prepare them in other ways for higher education and for the workplace. What does it take for teachers to handle this challenge? We must be clear about what teachers have to understand about language learning and teaching if they are to work effectively with their students. We have argued that basic coursework in educational linguistics is essential—the bare minimum for preparing teachers for today's schools.

# Glossary

| | |
|---|---|
| Cognate | A word related in form, meaning, and **etymology** to a word in another language |
| Dialect | A language variety in which sounds, grammar, and vocabulary identify speakers according to region or social class |
| Digraph | A letter combination that signals one sound, e.g., *th* |
| Discourse | A language structure longer than a sentence |
| Etymology | (a) the study of the historical origins of words; (b) with reference to a particular word, its historical origin(s) |
| Grapheme | The smallest unit of a written language, e.g., *t* |
| Indo-European languages | A family of related languages including English, thought to have originated in the Caucasus |
| Interlocutor | Participant in a discourse |
| Lexicon | The vocabulary of a language |
| Locative | A term that expresses location |
| Morpheme | The smallest meaning-bearing language structure, e.g., *dog, -ly* |
| Orthography | Conventions for spelling |
| Perlocutionary effect | Intended effects of a stretch of language, e.g., persuasion |
| Phoneme | The smallest meaning-distinguishing structure of the sound system, e.g., for English, [s] [š], *see, she* |
| Phonology | The system of rules for manipulating sounds in a language |
| Phraseology | Typical organization of words in a particular language into phrases and longer expressions |

# Acknowledgements

The authors are grateful to colleagues who contributed comments on an earlier version of this paper and supplied examples: Carolyn Temple Adger, Eve Agee, Kathleen Brown, Maria Carlo, Donna Christian, Charles J. Fillmore, Peg Griffin, Marita Hopmann, Joy Kreeft Peyton, Nicolas Zavala, and the participants in Lily Wong Fillmore's Fall 1998 Language Studies for Educators course, especially Laura Alamillo, Maren Aukerman, Marco Bravo, Laura Ruth Johnson, Nathan Keene, and Betty Pazmiño.

# Notes

[1] This is where the problem lies. Most people recognize that there can be considerable differences across individuals in ability, but not all cultures treat them differently in school. In most Asian societies, for example, children are placed in heterogeneous classrooms and are expected to learn the same curriculum, irrespective of any differences in ability. Those who need more help dealing with the materials get more help rather than an entirely different curriculum.

[2] There are cultures (Wong Fillmore's for one) in which children are not told what their mother's name is, and if a child were somehow to learn it, she would never speak it or acknowledge even that she had such information.

[3] We are grateful to Mary Eunice Romero for this reference. Popovi Da, a Pueblo leader, commenting on the relationship between the individual and the community, wrote: "Each person in Indian [Pueblo] society is born into his place in the community, which brings with it duties and responsibilities which he must perform throughout his life. Each member, old as well as young, has an important part to play in the organization of the tribe. . . . To work closely with the community gives strength and continuity to our culture and shows itself by the individual putting himself into the group, and putting the good of the group above his own desires" (1969).

[4] Richard Rodriguez (1982) offers a revealing account of what happens when parents are advised to switch to a language they do not speak easily or well for the sake of their children. He describes how the lively chatter at dinnertime was transformed into silence and how the silences in his home grew as the parents withdrew from participation in the lives of the children after teachers told them that the continued use of Spanish in the home was preventing the children from learning English.

[5] In her remarkable autobiography, first published in 1945, Jade Snow Wong (1989) describes how teachers, from elementary school through college, helped her find her way and her voice as an American scholar, writer, and artist without forfeiting her Chinese language and culture.

[6] National statistics for students designated limited English proficient (LEP) are hard to obtain and rarely up to date (see, for example, Hopstock & Bucaro, 1993). State education agencies (SEAs) report numbers of LEP students, but the criteria used to identify them vary across states, making comparisons difficult. The most recent national analysis of LEP student data reported by SEAs (Macias, 1998) reports a total enrollment of 3,378,861 LEP students, with 1,381,393 reported for California (41% of the national total). California's State Department of Education reported a total of 1,406,166 LEP students in California out of a total national LEP student enrollment of 5,727,303 (24.6%) for school year 1997-98 (California Department of Education, 2001).

# References

Aitchison, J. (1994). *Words in the mind: An introduction to the mental lexicon.* Oxford: Blackwell.

August, D., & Hakuta, K. (Eds). (1997). *Improving schooling for language minority children: A research agenda.* Washington, DC: National Academy Press.

Beck, I., McKeown, M. G., & Omanson, R. C. (1987). The effects and uses of diverse vocabulary instructional techniques. In M. G. McKeown & M. E. Curtis (Eds.), *The nature of vocabulary acquisition* (pp. 147–163). Hillsdale, NJ: Erlbaum.

Boggs, S. T. (1972). The meaning of narratives and questions to Hawaiian children. In C. B. Cazden, V. P. John, & D. Hymes (Eds.), *Functions of language in the classroom* (p. 299–330). New York: Teachers College Press.

California State Department of Education. (2001). *English learner (EL)** students and enrollment in California public schools, 1993 through 2001.* Retrieved July 2, 2002, from http://www.cde.ca.gov/demographics/REPORTS/statewide/lepstpct.htm

California State University. (1999). *Fall 1998 – fall 1999 remediation systemwide.* Retrieved July 2, 2002, from www.asd.calstate.edu/remrates/remrates98f-sys.htm

Collier, V. P. (1992). A synthesis of studies examining long-term language minority student data on academic achievement. *Bilingual Research Journal, 16,* 187–212.

Collier, V. P., & Thomas, W. P. (1989). How quickly can immigrants become proficient in school English? *Journal of Educational Issues of Language Minority Students, 5,* 26–38.

Cummins, J. (1981a). Age on arrival and immigrant second language learning in Canada: A reassessment. *Applied Linguistics, 2,* 132–149.

Cummins, J. (1981b). The role of primary language development in promoting educational success for language minority students. In California State Department of Education (Ed.), *Schooling and language minority students: A theoretical framework* (pp. 3-50). Los Angeles: California State University; Evaluation, Dissemination, and Assessment Center.

Cummins, J. (1984). *Bilingualism and special education: Issues in assessment and pedagogy.* Clevedon, England: Multilingual Matters.

Daniels, P., & Bright, W. (1996). *The world's writing systems.* New York: Oxford University Press.

Davison, A., & Kantor, R. (1982). On the failure of readability formulas to define readable texts: A case study from adaptations. *Reading Research Quarterly, 17*(2), 187-209.

Delpit, L. (1997). Ebonics and culturally responsive instruction. *Rethinking Schools, 12*(1), 6-7, 35.

Fillmore, L. W. (1982). Instructional language as linguistic input: Second language learning in classrooms. In L. C. Wilkinson (Ed.), *Communication in the classroom.* New York: Academic Press.

Fillmore, L. W. (1991). Second language learning in children: A model of language learning in social context. In E. Bialystok (Ed.), *Language processing by bilingual children* (pp. 49-69). New York: Cambridge University Press.

Fillmore, L. W. (1992). Learning a language from learners. In C. Kramsch & S. McConnell-Ginet (Eds.), *Text and context: Cross-disciplinary perspectives on language study.* Lexington, MA: D. C. Heath.

Fillmore, L. W. (1999, February). *The class of 2002: Will everyone be there?* Paper presented at the Alaska State Department of Education, Anchorage.

Fillmore, L. W. (in press). Language in education. In E. Finegan & J. Rickford (Eds.), *Language in the USA.* Cambridge: Cambridge University Press.

Gebhard, M. L. (2000). *Reconceptualizing classroom second language acquisition as an instructional phenomenon.* Unpublished doctoral dissertation, University of California at Berkeley.

Goals 2000: Educate America Act of 1994, Pub. L. No. 103–227, Title 20, § 5801 *et seq.*

González, J., & Darling–Hammond, L. (1997). *New concepts for new challenges: Professional development for teachers of immigrant youth.* McHenry, IL, and Washington, DC: Delta Systems and Center for Applied Linguistics.

Hakuta, K. (2001). *Key policy milestones and directions in the education of English language learners.* Paper prepared for the Rockefeller Foundation Symposium, Leveraging Change: An Emerging Framework for Education Equity, Washington, DC. Retrieved July 2, 2002, from http://www.stanford.edu/~hakuta/Docs/rockefeller/Rockefeller.htm

Heath, S. B. (1983). *Ways with words: Language, life, and work in communities and classrooms.* New York: Cambridge.

Hopstock, P. J., & Bucaro, B. J. (1993). *A review and analysis of estimates of the LEP student population.* Arlington, VA: Development Associates, Special Issues Analysis Center.

Hoyle, S. M., & Adger, C. T. (1998). Introduction. In S. M. Hoyle & C. T. Adger (Eds.), *Kids talk: Strategic language use in later childhood* (pp. 3–22). New York: Oxford.

Klesmer, H. (1994). Assessment and teacher perceptions of ESL student achievement. *English Quarterly, 26*(3), 8-11.

Long, M. H. (1985). Input and second language acquisition theory. In S. M. Gass & C. G. Madden (Eds.), *Input in second language acquisition* (pp. 377-393). Rowley, MA: Newbury.

Macias, R. F. (1998). *Summary report of the survey of the states' limited English proficient students and available educational programs and services, 1996-1997.* Washington, DC: National Clearinghouse for Bilingual Education.

McCabe, A. (1995). *Chameleon readers: Teaching children to appreciate all kinds of good stories.* New York: McGraw-Hill.

Merriman, W. E., & Kutlesic, V. (1993). Bilingual and monolingual children's use of two lexical acquisition heuristics. *Applied Linguistics, 14*, 229-49.

Michaels, S. (1981). Sharing time: Children's narrative styles and differential access to literacy. *Language in Society, 10*, 423-442.

Miller, G. A. (1976). *Spontaneous apprentices: Children and language.* New York: Seabury Press.

Miller, G. A. (1987). How children learn words. In F. Marshall (Ed), *Proceedings of the third eastern conference on linguistics.* Columbus: The Ohio State University.

Milner, B., Martin, J., & Evans, P. (1998). *Core science* (Key Concepts). Cambridge, England: Cambridge.

Murnane, R. J., & Levy, F. (1996). *Teaching the new basic skills: Principles for educating children to thrive in a changing economy.* New York: Free Press.

Oakes, J. (1985). *Keeping track: How schools structure inequality.* New Haven, CT: Yale University Press.

Oller, J. (1992) Language testing research: Lessons applied to LEP students and programs. In *Proceedings of the second national research symposium on limited English proficient student issues: Focus on evaluation and measurement* (Vol. 1, pp. 43-123). Washington, DC: U.S. Department of Education.

Olsen, L., Jaramillo, A., McCall-Perez, A., & White, J. (1999). *Igniting change for immigrant students: Portraits of three high schools.* Oakland, CA: California Tomorrow.

Ortiz, A. (1992). Assessing appropriate and inappropriate referral systems for LEP special education students. In *Proceedings of the second national research symposium on limited English proficient student issues: Focus on evaluation and measurement* (Vol. 1, pp. 315-342). Washington, DC: U.S. Department of Education.

Philips, S. U. (1993). *The invisible culture: Communication in the classroom and community on the Warm Springs Indian Reservation* (2nd ed.). New York: Free Press.

Pica, T. (1996). Second language learning through interaction: Multiple perspectives. *Working Papers in Educational Linguistics, 12,* 1-22.

Pinker, S. (1999). *Words and rules: The ingredients of language.* New York: Perseus.

Popovi Da. (1969). Indian values. *Journal of the Southwest Association of Indian Affairs,* 15-19.

Pressley, M. (1998). *Reading instruction that works: The case for balanced teaching.* New York: Guilford Press.

Ramírez, J. D., Pasta, D. J., Yuen, S., Billings, D. K., & Ramey, D. R. (1991). *Final report: Longitudinal study of structured immersion strategy, early-exit, and late-exit transitional bilingual education programs for language minority children.* San Mateo, CA: Aguirre International.

Rodriguez, R. (1982). *Hunger of memory: The autobiography of Richard Rodriguez.* Toronto and New York: Bantam.

Ruddell, R. B., & Unrau, N. J. (1997). The role of responsive teaching in focusing reader attention and developing reader motivation. In J. T. Guthrie & A. Wigfield (Eds.), *Reading engagement: Motivating readers through integrated instruction.* Newark, DE: International Reading Association.

Scarcella, R. (in press). *Key issues in accelerating English language development.* Berkeley: University of California Press.

Schmida, M. (1996). *"I don't understand what she be saying:"* Reconsidering the interlanguage and semilingual theories and explanations for first language loss and limited SLA. Unpublished manuscript, University of California at Berkeley.

Schmida, M. (in preparation). *Second language learning and peer identity.* Doctoral dissertation, University of California at Berkeley.

Schmida, M., & Chiang, Y. S. D. (1999). Language identity and language ownership: Linguistic conflicts of first year writing students. In L. Harklau, K. Losey, & M. Siegal (Eds.), *Generation 1.5 meets college composition: Issues in the teaching of writing to U.S. educated learners of ESL.* Mahwah, NJ: Erlbaum.

Smitherman, G. (1977). *Talkin and testifyin: The language of Black America.* Detroit: Wayne State University Press.

Snow, C. E., Burns. M. S., & Griffin, P. (Eds.). (1998). *Preventing reading difficulties in young children.* Washington, DC: National Academy Press.

Valdés, G. (1996). *Respeto: Bridging the differences between culturally diverse families and schools: An ethnographic portrait.* New York: Teachers College Press.

Wong, J. S. (1945/1989). *Fifth Chinese daughter.* Seattle: University of Washington Press.

Zentella, A. C. (1997). *Growing up bilingual.* Malden, MA: Blackwell.

Zuengler, J., & Cole, K. (2000, March). *Negotiating the high school mainstream: Language learners joining the talk in subject matter classes.* Paper presented at the annual meeting of the American Association for Applied Linguistics, Vancouver, BC.

# Chapter Two

# Language and Early Childhood Programs

Sue Bredekamp
Council for Early Childhood Professional Recognition

In "What Teachers Need to Know About Language," Lily Wong Fillmore and Catherine Snow have made another significant contribution to the field of education. With an undergraduate degree in English, graduate degrees in education, and course work in linguistics and the teaching of reading, I was both surprised and embarrassed at how little of the knowledge they call for I had learned, currently remember, or readily use in my work. More to the point, as an early childhood educator who has dedicated much of my professional life to improving the quality of programs that serve children in the earliest years of life, I was disturbed by how unattainable Fillmore and Snow's vision appears to be for my field.

Considerable evidence now exists that high-quality early childhood education programs can have long-lasting positive consequences for children's success in school and later in life, especially for children from low-income families (Barnett, 1995; Campbell & Ramey, 1995; Frede, 1995; Schweinhart, Barnes, & Weikart, 1993). However, such high-quality programs are not available for all children who need them. In fact, only about 15% of child care centers are judged to be of good or excellent quality. Almost 60% are considered mediocre, and another 15% to 20% are deemed inadequate or even harmful (Cost, Quality, and Child Outcomes Study Team, 1995).

A recent study of a random sample of Head Start programs found that, while none of the programs was inadequate, quality varied among the programs, and support for language and literacy learning was weak in many of them. Not surprisingly, children in the better quality programs out-performed children in lower quality programs on measures of learning and development (U.S. Department of Health and Human Services, 1998). In the better quality programs, children's expressive language skills approached or matched those of their middle-class counterparts, although, overall, Head Start children's scores were below national norms.

Recently, the U. S. Department of Education released the first data from the Early Childhood Longitudinal Study, which will follow a nationally representative cohort of 22,000 children from kindergarten through fifth grade (West, Denton, & Germino-Hausken, 2000). Data gathered on skills and knowledge at entrance to kindergarten demonstrated that, while most children were ready for school, social class and other group differences were already evident at this early stage. This finding suggests that even kindergarten is too late to intervene to narrow the achievement gap. What is needed are high-quality early childhood education programs, which have great potential for preventing later school failure, particularly if they place a strong emphasis on language development. However, the potential of early childhood education is far from being achieved.

In this chapter, I describe the context within which early childhood education takes place in the United States. I then identify the key language issues that teachers of young children are confronted with every day. Some of these issues differ from those addressed by Fillmore and Snow, who focus on school-age children. Early childhood is usually defined as birth through age 8, but for the purposes of this chapter, I address issues for teachers of children from birth to age 5.

# Early Childhood Education in Context

Early childhood programs operate in a variety of settings, both public and private, under a range of state standards, all of which are minimal. Unlike the K-12 educational system, in which certified teachers who hold baccalaureate degrees are the norm, early childhood programs are often staffed by teachers with minimal qualifications. As a result, 3- and 4-year-old children in the United States are enrolled in programs staffed by teachers with varying professional credentials. For example, a preschool child in Texas may attend a public school prekindergarten with a certified teacher, a Head Start program with a teacher who has a Child Development Associate (CDA) credential that requires 120 clock hours of formal professional education, or a child care center where the teacher must have only 8 clock hours of preservice training. (Head Start recently raised the teacher qualification requirement, and by 2003, 50% of their teachers must have at least an associate's degree in the field of early childhood education.) In addition, the younger the child, the less qualified the adult caregiver often is. This situation is particularly disturbing because the earliest years of life are prime for learning language.

Another complicating factor is that the content of early childhood teacher preparation varies greatly depending on state licensing standards for teachers. It is only within the last decade that the majority of states have had specialized licensure for early childhood teachers, and among those states are 12 different configurations of licensing based on the age range that a teacher is prepared to teach (Ratcliff, Cruz, & McCarthy, 1999). A number of states have an early childhood license that begins at kindergarten, which means that there is no baccalaureate-level preparation specific to serving children from birth through age 4. Many child care teachers attend associate-degree-granting institutions that offer majors in early childhood, but these programs do not provide the depth and breadth of language preparation outlined by Fillmore and Snow. Language development is usually addressed as part of a larger course on child development, and literacy may be a course of its own or part of a language arts strand.

More significant, however, is the level of compensation for early childhood teachers. Because of inferior compensation, programs cannot demand that teachers have strong qualifications, such as broad and deep knowledge of language. With no reliable third-party source of funding like public schools have (i.e., taxes), early childhood programs are subsidized by the teachers' low salaries and lack of benefits. Currently, teachers in programs for young children receive average salaries that are less than half those of public school teachers (Cost, Quality, and Child Outcomes Study Team, 1995). This lack of adequate compensation leads to high rates of staff turnover in early childhood programs and makes it virtually impossible to recruit and retain well-qualified, well-educated teachers.

A further complicating factor for early childhood programs is that they are being brought into the standards and accountability movement that has had a major impact on K-12 education over the last decade. States are adding prekindergarten standards and assessments, and Head Start is incorporating child outcomes data as part of its evaluation and accountability systems. Thus, very young children, including children whose home language is not English, are expected to demonstrate specific progress on identified learning outcomes, which always include language and early literacy objectives. This trend is positive in many ways, because it helps early childhood teachers focus on appropriate goals and encourages them to pay attention to individual children's progress, adapting instruction and experiences when necessary. Of course, there are also many potentially negative aspects to the standards and accountability trend, especially when children's individual rates of development and learning are ignored, or when it is not understood that their competencies were acquired in cultural and linguistic contexts that may not match those of the schools.

This brief but bleak portrait of the context of early childhood education suggests that Fillmore and Snow have presented us with a daunting challenge. The task of ensuring that every early childhood teacher is sufficiently knowledgeable about language becomes overwhelming in the context of minimal and uneven teacher qualifications, diverse preparation programs, and frequent staff turnover. Given the range of teacher qualifications, or the lack thereof, the minimum standard for knowledge about language that teachers should possess is difficult to set, particularly if it presupposes a teacher with a college degree. Moreover, there are other language issues confronting teachers working with young children that they have not addressed, a discussion of which follows.

# Why Do Early Childhood Teachers Need to Know More About Language?

The five teacher functions that Fillmore and Snow identify—communicator, educator, evaluator, educated human being, and agent of socialization—are all relevant for teachers working with young children. Some are particularly critical, because these earliest years of development are the foundation for so much that occurs later.

## Teacher as Communicator

The role of communicator or conversational partner is especially critical in the preschool years, the years during which a great deal of language acquisition occurs. While it is true that, as Fillmore and Snow point out, language is not fully formed by age 5 or 6, a considerable amount of significant language development has or should have occurred by then. Young children acquire language through interactions with more accomplished speakers of the language, such as parents, family members, and teachers, as well as other children. However, many teachers and caregivers of very young children persist in the view that there is no reason to talk to children who cannot talk back. In addition, certain child-rearing patterns and cultural perspectives lead to language interaction between adults and very young children that is quite different from the expectations of the school or program, as Fillmore and Snow describe. "To communicate successfully, teachers must know how to structure their own language output for maximum clarity. They must also have strategies for understanding what students are saying" (this volume, p. 10 ). This task is difficult enough when students are experienced users of language. However, when children are just learning to talk, the task of supporting each child's language acquisition and of understanding what they are trying to say can be quite a challenge. For instance, it is not uncommon to find a situation where a child's mother is the only person who can interpret the child's communications. When children are served in groups, the teacher's role as interlocutor becomes even more complex. As a former preschool teacher, I can attest to the fact that children whose language is more advanced are typically spoken to more often by adults. This leads to a vicious cycle in which those children who are lagging behind engage in less language interaction than they need, and those who need interaction less get more of it.

Virtually every early childhood teacher preparation program addresses the topic of language development. Unfortunately, what teacher candidates are likely to learn about is the continuum of language development from cooing and babbling to one-word utterances, and so on. This process is too often presented as though it is purely maturational. While maturation does play a part in language development, the role of experience and learning, especially within the social and cultural context, is much more significant. This dimension of language acquisition is not taught specifically, which leaves many teacher candidates with no idea of what their role is in supporting language development at various levels or of what to do when it does not proceed as expected. Fillmore and Snow provide an outstanding rationale for why teachers need to know about language, but the emphasis for teachers of young children needs to be slightly different. Early childhood teachers need to talk with children in ways that ensure that their language continues to develop, their vocabulary increases, and their grammar becomes more complex.

At the same time, effective language interactions vary with the age of the child. The way we speak to babies, such as the use of "motherese," is different from the way we interact with young toddlers—whose communications we may repeat or finish (e.g., Child: "Juice." Adult: "You want some orange juice?")—or with preschoolers, who need cognitively challenging language interaction and extended one-to-one conversation. Although this is not empirically documented, I have informally observed among teacher educators and teachers that teacher candidates in professional preparation programs are not actually taught how to talk with young children in ways that promote optimal language development. I personally believe that talking to young children is a very difficult task. Most adults tend to interrogate children (e.g., What color is this? What letter is this?) rather than interact with them. Even in ostensible conversations, adults tend to answer for children when responses are not immediately forthcoming. For babies, toddlers, and preschool-aged children whose home language is not English, the challenges and questions are even more complex. Research shows that moving children into English too soon can precipitate loss of the home language, which in turn disrupts family relationships and cultural and personal identity (Fillmore, 1991).

Ideally, the goal is to support development of both English and the home language at the same time, but this requires hiring staff who are accomplished speakers of both languages. Given the staffing problems identified earlier, this is rarely achieved. Parents typically prefer that teachers and caregivers come from their own cultural and linguistic community, a goal that is often met through family child care arrangements or Head Start. This preference may lead to hiring adults who do not speak English or who speak vernacular dialects of English. Such choices may promote and respect the home language, but they do not provide language models that support the acquisition of Standard English. Other families may want to move their children into English right away, which can result in negative consequences for the home language or can prevent children from acquiring a strong foundation in either their native language or English. For teachers of young children, the role of conversational partner—perhaps their most important role in language development—overlaps considerably with the role of educator. Early childhood teacher preparation must emphasize the particular function of the adult's role in building language acquisition in the practical sense as well as the theoretical.

## Teacher as Evaluator

More and more, early childhood teachers are thrust into the role of evaluators of children's language. This has always been a very difficult role, because it involves attempting to identify children who may have developmental delays or disabilities. When young children are in the early stages of acquiring language, it is especially difficult to obtain valid and reliable data on their capabilities. Is performance variance attributable to normal, individual variation in rates of development, to experiential variation that is relatively easy to remediate, or to an actual delay? The idea that every evaluation or assessment is actually a language assessment is also difficult for inexperienced, untrained evaluators to grasp, especially when they do not speak the language of the children being assessed. Head Start mandates that children with disabilities or developmental delays make up 10% of all programs; of that 10%, a large majority are identified as having language delays. No one really knows how many of these children are appropriately identified, but children whose home language is not English or is not Standard English are undoubtedly over-represented.

## Teacher as Educator and Educated Human Being

Teachers of young children need to be generalists in their knowledge of the world because children are interested in everything that goes on around them. They want to know about insects, flora, fauna, weather, space travel, families, dinosaurs, food, jobs, construction, transportation, and why anything and everything happens! This does not mean that early childhood teachers must have every fact at their disposal, but it does mean that they need to have the extended vocabulary, curiosity, and skills to find out what they need to know to answer children's questions. The role of teacher of young children is complex, but it certainly includes being a key informant and co-investigator. The poor salaries and inferior qualifications of teachers of young children reflect the persistent notion that these teachers do not need to know very much. In fact, the roles early childhood teachers need to fulfill in the area of language alone—not to mention literacy, mathematics, science, social development, and many others—belie this myth.

### Teacher as Agent of Socialization

Socialization and language are two interrelated areas of development in the early years of life. By school entrance, the process of socialization is well underway. However, when children are served in programs outside of the home beginning as babies, toddlers, and preschoolers, the socialization process is occurring simultaneously in two environments. The need to respect home languages and cultures is especially important. But how to convey this attitude while at the same time promoting the acquisition of Standard English is problematic. Even well-qualified teachers ask, "How do I respect home language and support English language learning? When and how should English be introduced? How much do I need to know about culture(s)? What do I do when there are many different languages and cultures in the programs or when parents do not agree?" There are no simple answers to these questions. Instead, teachers must become skilled communicators and negotiators with families; they must be sufficiently knowledgeable to become skilled professional decision-makers (Bredekamp & Copple, 1997).

## What Should the Early Childhood Classroom Teacher Know?

The issues that Fillmore and Snow discuss would be enlightening for most early childhood teachers and teacher candidates. Often, knowing what you do not already know is the best place to start a journey of discovery. For early childhood educators, I believe the focus should be on what they need to know and be able to do. What teachers need to know about language is important, but it is not as important as what they do with children.

## Oral Language

Although oral language development is a primary goal in early childhood programs, the learning experiences and teaching strategies provided do not always support this goal. Perhaps the most thorough observational study of what goes on in preschools was funded by the U.S. Department of Education (Layzer, Goodson, & Moss, 1993). The study describes the experiences of 4-year-old children from low-income families in three types of programs: Head Start, Chapter 1-funded prekindergartens, and child care centers. Findings were not generalizable by program type because sites were not randomly selected. However, acceptable levels of quality were maintained in all three program types, with Head Start consistently rated highest. Observers spent one week in each classroom to get a comprehensive picture of what life is like in preschool. Many findings were positive, but others were of concern. A wide variety of activities was generally available, with more than half the children's time spent in experiences designed to foster cognitive growth, but 20% of their time was spent in routines. Surprisingly, more than 25% of the classrooms did not have a story time, either for the whole group or for smaller groups.

The study also provided a picture of teacher–child interactions. Teachers spent about two thirds of their time involved with children, but just 25% of that time was spent in teaching activities; 20% was spent controlling or managing children's behavior. Interacting with children on an individual basis was rare for teachers, who spent only 10% of their time in individual interaction. Most disturbing, more than 30% of all the children across all classrooms had no individual interaction with a teacher, although the number varied by classroom from a few to the majority. In 12% of the classrooms, more than half the children received no individual attention over two observational periods (Layzer, Goodson, & Moss, 1993).

The finding that a quarter of the classrooms did not even have one story time in a week is shocking. Given the value of storybook reading for vocabulary development and comprehension, not to mention that children usually love reading books, omitting story time is inexcusable. I can only speculate that teachers saw story time as strictly a whole-group activity that they had diffi-culty managing and therefore avoided.

The most common form of communication with children was commanding (33.7%), followed by explaining (33%) and questioning (16.3%). Given the recent emphasis on language and early literacy experiences in preschool, these findings might not be replicated today. Nevertheless, they have important implications for teacher education programs. Early childhood teachers need to know that one-to-one, extended, cognitively challenging conversations are necessary, and they need to know how to engage in such communication even with reluctant talkers. They need to know not only how the lexicon is acquired but also how to engage in practices that support vocabulary acquisi-tion. They also need to know how to engage in story reading and many other early literacy experiences, such as those that promote phonological awareness and prepare children for later success in reading (Dickinson & Smith, 1994; Snow, Burns, & Griffin, 1998).

If the picture of what goes on in preschools is enlightening, then it is also important to take a look at children's language development at home. A sem-inal observational study of children's early language experiences in their homes gathered an enormous amount of data over the first 3 years of chil-dren's lives (Hart & Risley, 1995). The title of the book reporting the results mirrors the findings: *Meaningful Differences in the Everyday Experience of Young American Children*. Significant differences between social-class groups were found both in quantity and quality of children's early language experiences. The researchers compared the language interactions in professional-level, working-class, and welfare-recipient families. They found that by 3 years of age, the number of words that children had been exposed to in adult–child interactions ranged from 10 million in welfare families to more than 40 mil-lion in professional families. They also found that the quality of interactions varied greatly, with welfare families responding negatively to their child's lan-guage initiations 80% of the time, and professional families responding posi-tively 80% of the time. At age 4, children's language patterns mirrored those of their families.

I present these two contexts for language use—program and home—to demonstrate the extreme challenge confronting early childhood educators.

With increasing emphasis on school readiness, gaps in vocabulary size on arrival at school can imperil children's academic futures. Thus we need to think about how best to structure preschool programs to ensure vocabulary development for all children. Kindergarten is much too late to address the language development trajectories of the children from the welfare and working-class families described in Hart and Risley's study. Earlier intervention is needed to prevent a gap from arising so that no one appears at the school door lacking the language skills that schools expect. Preschool programs must work to promote language development in all children. Given that children acquire language best in meaningful contexts, through conversational interactions and through encounters with written language, these must be the focus of instruction for teacher candidates.

Children also need time for social interaction and play with peers, which provide excellent opportunities for language acquisition. But here again, the potential of the early childhood context is limited by its reality. Too often, opportunity for peer interaction is not provided at preschool, because young children are perceived to need more instruction from the teacher. Without external funding, early childhood programs are economically segregated so that children interact only with members of their own social, economic, and cultural group. Children who need them most often lack peer models of school-sanctioned language. In addition, children who are acquiring English as a second language need to interact with native-speaker peers, but often they do not because they are served within their own language community, and the teacher is the only one who speaks English.

Fillmore and Snow's discussion of vernacular dialects of English is excellent. This is an issue that has generated great controversy and very little light. It is easy to agree with every point they raise on the issue, yet still be left searching for clarity on how to carry out what they recommend. Their discussion also raises frustrating questions. We assume that young children need teachers who speak their language. If this applies to vernacular dialects, how do children learn Standard English? In a racist and classist society, the more successful minority group members are those who can code-switch—that is, those who can converse in the language of the dominant culture but never lose their connection to or their ability to communicate in their own community and cultural group. Code-switching seems to be the product of family instruction, but is there an effective role for educational institutions to play? Also, how do mainstream institutions, including child care and preschool programs, even raise the issue without being perceived as racist and classist?

## Written Language

Much of what Fillmore and Snow address under written language is less applicable to younger children, and yet the knowledge is valuable for their teachers. The topic that they do not address in detail is phonics instruction and its relationship to precursors in phonological and phonemic awareness. These are topics that early childhood teachers need to know more about, including appropriate ways for teaching young children. Mandates regarding phonics instruction are increasing, and this instruction is being thrust upon younger and younger children. Most early childhood teachers do not have sufficient training in ways to support children's early literacy learning. We tend to tell them what not to do rather than what to do. If we advocate a balanced approach, they are left wondering what constitutes balance. If we tell them that simplistic phonics approaches are inadvisable in teaching English reading (as Fillmore and Snow say and with which I agree), we must also tell them how much phonics children do need, how to know which children need more or less explicit phonics instruction, and when to stop teaching phonics to which children. Given the political climate surrounding phonics instruction, as well as the lack of research to answer these questions, this may be an unreasonable request. Nevertheless, it is what early childhood teachers need to know about written language.

## Courses Teachers Need to Take

The list of courses that Fillmore and Snow recommend is exhaustive, although they indicate that the content does not need to be structured into individual courses. The study of cultural and linguistic diversity should be integrated throughout an early childhood teacher education program. Therefore, some of what they recommend might be addressed in multiple courses across diverse discipline areas (e.g., working with families, social-emotional development) (National Association for the Education of Young Children et al., 1996). I believe the two areas of study that are essential for teachers of young children are language development, including adults' role in supporting it, and second language learning and teaching that addresses the youngest age groups, including preverbal infants.

The more pressing question, however, is, Who will teach such courses? I remember taking a linguistics class as part of my education course work and seeing no connection in what I was learning in the course to my future role as a teacher. In fact, it was one of the only courses I took that I did not really like. Unless these courses are taught by individuals who are educational linguists and who can connect learning to the real work of teachers, the study of these topics will neither inspire teachers nor improve teaching and learning for children. Achieving this goal will be even harder for teachers of young children.

## Conclusion

Educators are indebted to Lily Wong Fillmore and Catherine Snow for the series of challenges they present here. I began this chapter by describing the context of early childhood education, which presents a discouraging picture. However, knowing what teachers need to know about language (which is only one area of the curriculum, albeit a critical one) demands that the issue of teacher qualifications in early childhood education be addressed. Teachers of young children must obtain more education, better compensation, and greater respect. Their role in supporting children's language acquisition alone is the "bare minimum" (Fillmore & Snow, this volume, p. 43 ) of what they have to contribute to children's well-being and future potential.

# References

Barnett, W. S. (1995). Long-term effects of early childhood programs on cognitive and school outcomes. *The Future of Children, 5*, 25–50.

Bredekamp, S., & Copple, C. (Eds.). (1997). *Developmentally appropriate practice in early childhood programs* (Rev. ed.). Washington, DC: National Association for the Education of Young Children.

Campbell, F., & Ramey, C. (1995). Cognitive and school outcomes for high-risk African-American students at middle adolescence: Positive effects of early intervention. *American Educational Research Journal, 32*, 743–72.

Cost, Quality, & Child Outcomes Study Team. (1995). *Cost, quality, and child outcomes in child care centers* (Public Report, 2nd ed.). Denver: University of Colorado at Denver, Economics Department.

Dickinson, D., & Smith, M. (1994). Long-term effects of preschool teachers' book readings on low-income children's vocabulary and story comprehension. *Reading Research Quarterly, 29*, 104–22.

Fillmore, L. W. (1991). When learning a second language means losing the first. *Early Childhood Research Quarterly, 6*, 323–46.

Frede, E. (1995). The role of program quality in producing early childhood program benefits. *The Future of Children, 5*, 115–32.

Hart, B., & Risley, T. (1995). *Meaningful differences in the everyday experience of young American children*. Baltimore: Brookes.

Layzer, J., Goodson, B., & Moss, M. (1993). *Life in preschool: Volume one of an observational study of early childhood programs for disadvantaged four-year-olds.* Cambridge, MA: Abt Associates.

National Association for the Education of Young Children, Division for Early Childhood of the Council for Exceptional Children, and National Board for Professional Teaching Standards. (1996). *Guidelines for preparation of early childhood professionals.* Washington, DC. National Association for the Education of Young Children.

Ratcliff, N., Cruz, J., & McCarthy, J. (1999). *Early childhood teacher education licensure patterns and curriculum guidelines: A state-by-state analysis.* Washington, DC: Council for Professional Recognition.

Schweinhart, L. J., Barnes, H.V., & Weikart, D. P. (1993). *Significant benefits: The High/Scope Perry Preschool study through age 27.* Ypsilanti, MI: High/Scope Press.

Snow, C., Burns, S., & Griffin, P. (1998). *Preventing reading difficulties in young children.* Washington, DC: National Academy Press.

U.S. Department of Health and Human Services. (1998). *Head Start program performance measures: Second progress report.* Washington, DC: Author.

West, J., Denton, K., & Germino-Hausken, E. (2000). *America's kindergartners: Findings from the early childhood longitudinal study, kindergarten class of 1998-99, Fall 1998.* Washington, DC: U.S. Department of Education, National Center for Education Statistics.

# Chapter Three

# Educating Teachers About Language

Leonard Baca
Kathy Escamilla
University of Colorado

We are in strong agreement with Fillmore and Snow's argument regarding the need for all teachers to gain a deeper understanding of language, linguistics, and sociolinguistics. The need is especially urgent for those who teach second language learners. We commend Fillmore and Snow for expanding the dialogue about teaching second language learners beyond the usual focus on beginning-level students. Much work needs to be done to move intermediate second language learners toward full academic proficiency in English.

Our response to the Fillmore and Snow chapter comes from the perspective of bilingual/ESL teacher educators caught between an ideal conceptualization of what teachers need to know about language to do their work well and the real world demands of state policies that are increasingly limiting the amount of course work that can be required in initial teacher certification programs. These policies diminish the opportunity for teacher educators to lead teacher candidates in building the knowledge and skills they need to be effective in our schools. In this chapter, we point out several actions that Fillmore and Snow call for that we believe to be essential, and we propose an addition to the course work that they outline. We then explore a way of addressing the limitations on teacher training imposed by state policies.

## Declining Knowledge About the English Language

Fillmore and Snow present a very strong rationale for why teachers need to know more about language and how languages work. In their call for training in the areas of linguistics and sociolinguistics, they refer to the country's shifting demographics, including the tremendous increase in the number of English language learners in the public schools. They also articulate important language-related roles that teachers play and the linguistic knowledge that teachers need for these roles. Beyond that, Fillmore and Snow place the study of language in historical perspective. They point out that today's teachers have not generally been required to study the English language—or any language—in depth. We are referring here to a formal study of the history and structure of English or other languages. One of us remembers taking 4 years of Latin in high school. It did not result in a high level of Latin fluency but did lead to a much better understanding of English grammar and syntax. Few schools offer Latin today. It is also the case, unfortunately, that too few of them require the study of foreign languages or in-depth study of the grammar of English. Language requirements have been relaxed at both the K–12 and university levels, a trend that has contributed to the problem of inadequate teacher preparation with regard to knowledge about language.

Given the declining support for the formal study of language, English grammar, and linguistics at all levels of education, it becomes clear that solving the linguistic knowledge problem calls for a systemic approach beyond the domain of teacher preparation. Other areas of higher education have an important role to play. Foreign language requirements and English language requirements need to be strengthened throughout the university. Likewise, public school requirements in English language arts and other languages must be revisited and strengthened as well. Moreover, as Fillmore and Snow so forcefully state, the study of language must be expanded beyond the once traditional attention to grammar to include sociolinguistic topics, such as patterns of language use in different communities and social settings, that can help teachers understand students' language use at school. Addressing these issues will require more than a simple return to the language study traditions of the past. It will require significant updates in teacher preparation and teacher development syllabi.

## Standards-Based Education

Fillmore and Snow point out that one obvious vehicle for addressing issues concerning knowledge about language is the standards movement that lies at the heart of current educational reform efforts (Goals 2000: Educate America Act, 1994; Improving America's Schools Act, 1994). The content and performance standards developed by the states and professional organizations can contribute to the expansion and improvement of the study of English for both native and nonnative speakers.

Initially, discussions about standards-based education focused on K–12 education, but it did not take long for the standards movement to affect teacher education. In 1986, the Task Force on Teaching as a Profession, of the Carnegie Forum on Education and the Economy, published *A Nation Prepared: Teachers for the 21st Century* (Carnegie Forum on Education and the Economy, 1986). That document detailed an eight-point action plan calling for higher standards for entering teachers (It also cited the need to recruit more minority teachers [Baca, Escamilla, & Carjuzaa, 1994]). In the same year, the Holmes Group, a teacher education reform group, published *Tomorrow's Teachers* (Holmes Group, 1986). This report dealt with the role of higher education in the preparation of teachers. It promoted higher standards and advised exploration of the issues confronting teachers and teacher education. It advocated the professionalization of the teaching force (Baca et al., 1994). Both of these reports focused on the content-area knowledge that future teachers need and de-emphasized knowledge related to pedagogy.

With respect to pedagogy, The Center for Research on Education, Diversity & Excellence (CREDE) has published a set of five standards for effective teaching and learning based on a comprehensive review of the literature and the consensus of multiple groups of educators and researchers (Tharp, 1997). These standards are highly relevant to the reform of teacher education and professional development for in-service teachers. Rueda (1998) has adapted them for use in professional development:

- Facilitate learning and development by involving leaders and participants jointly in productive activity.
- Promote learners' ability to participate in discourse on professional topics.

- Connect teaching and learning to the experiences and skills of participants.
- Challenge participants to develop complex solutions to problems.
- Engage participants in dialogue, especially in instructional conversations.

Dalton (1998) suggests that the term *standard* is to be understood in this context to signal its original meaning: the standard as the flag that leads the way, giving direction at the head of a procession. In that sense, these standards serve as basic guidelines or principles for guiding staff development and teacher education.

Clearly, there is an essential connection between teaching and standards for K–12 students (National Board for Professional Teaching Standards, 1989). If the new, challenging content and performance standards for K–12 students are to be achieved, a well-prepared teaching force is required. For that reason, the standards movement today is driving much of the reform in teacher education.

## Issues in Improving Teacher Education

In some locations, the standards movement has already shaped teacher preparation programs. A telling example is the state of Colorado, which adopted a new set of *Standards for Teacher Education* in May 2000 (Standards for Teacher Education, 2000). At present, all syllabi for teacher education classes are being prepared around the state's K–12 and teacher education standards, and each course must specifically address these standards. All candidates must complete their program within 4 years or 120 semester hours.

Revising the teacher preparation curriculum to reflect the standards does not resolve all of the issues associated with improving teaching and teacher education; in fact, the standards raise some new issues. Fillmore and Snow, as well as others (see, e.g., August & Hakuta, 1997, and McLaughlin & Shepard, 1995), have pointed out that the standards-based education movement has not adequately addressed the educational plight of two significant populations: K–12 students who are learning English as a second language and the teachers who teach these students. Indeed, in Colorado, the influential state teacher education standards do not include standards related to teaching diverse populations or English language learners.

Colorado's new standards place tight restrictions on teacher education programs. Teacher educators are being asked to teach more in less time: The mandate to prepare teachers in 120 semester hours represents a 20 semester hour reduction from previous requirements. Professors are struggling to incorporate all of the K-12 and teacher education standards into the limited number of semester hours. Further, future teachers must have an academic major; they cannot major in education. Majors in psychology, sociology, anthropology, and linguistics are discouraged, as the state prefers academic majors in disciplines that are taught in public schools, such as history, math, and science.

While university teacher education programs are addressing these new limits, Colorado school districts are facing numerous challenges in implementing standards-based educational programs—challenges that have implications for teacher education. Many of these challenges are linked to the growing number of ethnically, linguistically, and economically diverse students in K-12 classrooms in the state; a rapidly growing K-12 population; and the beginnings of a severe teacher shortage. This shortage is most severe in the areas of ESL and bilingual education. It is doubtful that teacher education programs in the state will be able to produce the number of teachers needed to address this shortage. As a result, many school districts in the state have had to employ teachers on emergency authorization and to create and support alternative licensure programs for these teachers. It also falls to school districts to help these teachers learn what they need to know about the standards and to support them as they implement standards in their classrooms.

Neither the changing K-12 population, nor the pending teacher shortage, nor the challenges of implementing standards-based reforms are unique to Colorado. Rather, they reflect national trends. The suggestions offered by Fillmore and Snow must be understood in the context of tremendous pressures on school districts and teacher education programs.

## The Language Knowledge Base

We are not suggesting that these heavy demands on teacher education and school districts mitigate the importance of Fillmore and Snow's arguments. To the contrary, their proposal provides an excellent framework for the set of teacher education courses that could lead to improved opportunities to learn for English language learners. We agree wholeheartedly that the knowledge base they propose should be included in teacher preparation programs for all teachers, not just those preparing to be bilingual or ESL teachers. But where and how do we fit this knowledge base and course work into our current pre-service teacher preparation programs, given new state mandates for less course work and more attention to the K–12 content standards? How do we fit an additional 21 units of course work into existing 30-unit degree programs for Master's students?

We do not mean to suggest that answering these questions should involve reducing either the breadth or the depth of the Fillmore and Snow proposal. In fact, rather than reduce or condense it, we suggest an addition to the topics they set out. We submit that teacher education programs must address the beliefs that teachers have about how second languages are learned and acquired. The impact of teachers' beliefs on their teaching practices has been well documented (Gonzales & Darling-Hammond, 1997; Houston, 1990; Pajares, 1992; Richardson, Anders, Tidwell, & Lloyd, 1991). McLaughlin (1992) outlines common teacher beliefs about second language acquisition and documents some myths and misconceptions about teaching English to second language learners:

**Myth 1: Children learn second languages quickly and easily, and they learn second languages faster than adults do.**

In fact, research supports the opposite conclusion: The adult is the better and faster learner of second languages. Language learning is complex and requires strong teacher support over several years (Bialystok & Hakuta, 1994; Birdsong & Molis, 2001).

**Myth 2: The younger the child, the more skilled he or she will be in acquiring the second language.**

Again, the research does not support this assumption. The only advantage the younger child has is the ability to develop more native-like pronunciation. Older children make more rapid progress in language acquisition because of their more advanced cognitive development (Bialystok & Hakuta, 1999; Flege, 1999; Snow, 1987).

Myth 3: The more time students spend in a context where English predominates, the more quickly they learn the language.

This is the assumption behind the support for Proposition 227 in California. Research, however, has shown that children who receive bilingual education acquire English language skills equivalent to those acquired by children who have been in English-only programs (Cummins, 1981; Hakuta, 2001; Ramirez, Yuen, & Ramey, 1991).

Myth 4: Children have acquired a second language once they are able to speak it.

Many teachers think that because an immigrant child speaks in English on the playground, that child is ready for an all-English curriculum. However, a child who is proficient in face-to-face social communication is not necessarily ready for the more abstract, disembedded use of language in academic contexts (August & Hakuta, 1997; Bialystok & Hakuta, 1994; Cummins, 2000).

Myth 5: All children learn additional languages in the same way.

While teachers may not say this, the curriculum in many schools reflects this unwarranted belief. However, the research in this area shows that there are differences across groups according to language and that there are differences within specific language groups. (See, e.g., Heath, 1983.)

In summary, it is important for all teachers to understand that second language learning takes longer, is harder and more complex, and involves a great deal more effort than they have been led to believe.

## Changing What Teachers Learn About Language

We suggest two general approaches to implementing Fillmore and Snow's suggestions for enhancing teacher expertise with regard to language: (1) increased support from professional organizations for reforming teacher education and (2) broad distribution of language information across teacher education courses and professional development programs for in-service teachers.

Although the standards train has already left the station, it is not too late to use this vehicle for improving the linguistic knowledge of teachers. Even though the opportunity to develop standards that address language knowledge comprehensively has been missed, it is not too late to challenge the standards-setting players to affect the standards implementation process with regard to the language and language learning issues for teachers that Fillmore and Snow raise.

Three influential language-related groups could assist with this effort: the National Council of Teachers of English (NCTE), Teachers of English to Speakers of Other Languages (TESOL), and the National Association for Bilingual Education (NABE). NCTE has established standards for what students need to know and be able to do with regard to understanding and using the English language in the public schools (National Council of Teachers of English and International Reading Association, 1996). The TESOL standards for preK–12 students (Teachers of English to Speakers of Other Languages, 1997) and the NABE standards for preparing bilingual/multicultural teachers (National Association for Bilingual Education, 1992) provide direction for improving teaching of second language learners in K-12 classrooms. Raising the standards here should produce high school graduates who have higher levels of English competency and greater knowledge about language before they go into teacher preparation programs. Higher standards at the K–12 level should also put pressure on higher education to strengthen the knowledge of language and linguistics required of teacher candidates who will address these standards when they enter the profession.

Another influential group is the National Council for the Accreditation of Teacher Education (NCATE). Donna Gollnick (this volume) describes that group's progress in developing teacher preparation standards for all teachers that include more in-depth knowledge of culture, the English language, and linguistics.

A practical approach to increasing teacher knowledge about language involves reconfiguring teacher preparation programs. Fillmore and Snow have proposed a comprehensive list of courses that would provide this knowledge. Adding the language courses is impractical in the context of the regular course requirements for either an undergraduate degree or a master's degree in education. One possible approach to addressing this problem is creating a new kind of master's degree in the area of bilingual education and ESL that would focus on the structure of English and on sociolinguistics. Teachers with this training could provide expertise to staff development programs in school districts.

But as we have emphasized, along with Fillmore and Snow, *all* teachers need to know much more about language. Thus we suggest a second, more general solution: distributing the recommended courses across the years of undergraduate and graduate education and through ongoing professional development for teachers. In that scenario, the training sequence might look like this:

Undergraduate teacher preparation would include these courses:

- Language Development
- Language and Cultural Diversity

Master's degrees in education would include these:

- Language and Linguistics
- Sociolinguistics for Educators in a Linguistically Diverse Society
- Second Language Learning and Teaching

Professional development programs would offer these courses:

- The Language of Academic Discourse
- Text Analysis and Language Understanding in Educational Settings

While not every teacher would end up taking the entire sequence of courses in this model, all teachers would have at least a basic foundation of the knowledge and skills necessary to promote their students' language development. Teachers who pursue master's degrees would have all of the recommended courses. Specialized teachers—especially bilingual and ESL teachers and perhaps literacy specialists—could address all of the recommended topics in redesigned classes.

As teacher educators, we recommend that this ambitious effort begin at the higher education level in the relevant content area courses. If bilingual and ESL educators took the lead, they could invite their colleagues in reading and English language arts education, as well as in English departments, to cooperate in this effort. In addition, a language and culture curriculum for professional development could be designed in collaboration with the staff development units in public school districts. This model could be developed, implemented, and refined over a period of several years.

Implementing the changes that Fillmore and Snow call for must proceed from a broad, systemic view of education, taking into account the kinds of knowledge about language that teacher candidates can be expected to have acquired, the state and status of the language and language learning standards for K-12 students, the emerging standards for teaching and teacher education, and the roles of professional associations and educational policy makers in standards implementation. Change must come at multiple levels, including the public schools and higher education.

# References

August, D., & Hakuta, K. (Eds.). (1997). *Improving schooling for language-minority children*. Washington, DC: National Academy Press.

Baca, L., Escamilla, K., & Carjuzaa, J. (1994). *Literacy: A redefinition*. New York: Erlbaum.

Bialystok, E., & Hakuta, K. (1994). *In other words: The science and psychology of second-language acquisition*. New York: Basic Books.

Bialystok, E., & Hakuta, K. (1999). Confounded age: Linguistic and cognitive factors in age differences for second language acquisition. In D. Birdsong (Ed.), *Second language acquisition and the critical period hypothesis* (pp. 161–181). Mahwah, NJ: Erlbaum.

Birdsong, D., & Molis, M. (2001). On the evidence for maturational effects in second language acquisition. *Journal of Memory and Language, 44*, 235-249.

Carnegie Forum on Education and the Economy. (1986). *A nation prepared: Teachers for the twenty-first century*. New York: Carnegie Corporation.

Cummins, J. (1981). The role of primary language development in promoting educational success for language minority students. In *Schooling and language minority students: A theoretical framework* (pp. 3-50). Los Angeles: California State University; Evaluation, Dissemination and Assessment Center.

Cummins, J. (2000). *Language, power and pedagogy*. Clevedon, England: Multilingual Matters.

Dalton, S. (1998). *Pedagogy matters: Standards for effective teaching practice* (Research Rep. No. 4). Washington, DC, and Santa Cruz, CA: Center for Research on Education, Diversity & Excellence.

Flege, J. E. (1999). Age of learning and second-language speech. In D. Birdsong (Ed.), *Second language acquisition and the critical period hypothesis* (pp. 101-131). Mahwah, NJ: Erlbaum.

Goals 2000: Educate America Act of 1994, Pub. L. No. 103-227, Title 20, § 5801 *et seq.*

Gonzales, J., & Darling-Hammond, L. (1997). *New concepts for new challenges: Professional development for teachers of immigrant youth.* McHenry, IL, and Washington, DC: Delta Systems and Center for Applied Linguistics.

Hakuta, K. (2001). *The education of language minority students: Testimony to the United States Commission on Civil Rights.* Retrieved July 2, 2002, from http://www.stanford.edu/~hakuta/Docs/CivilRightsCommission.htm

Heath, S. B. (1983). *Ways with words: Language, life, and work in communities and classrooms.* New York: Cambridge.

Holmes Group. (1986). *Tomorrow's teachers: A report of the Holmes Group.* East Lansing, MI: Author.

Houston, W. R. (Ed.). (1990). *Handbook of research on teaching.* New York: MacMillan.

Improving America's Schools Act of 1994, Pub. L. No. 103-382, § 7101 *et seq.*

McLaughlin, B. (1992). *Myths and misconceptions about second language learning: What every teacher needs to unlearn* (Educational Practice Rep. No. 5). Washington, DC, and Santa Cruz, CA: National Center for Research on Cultural Diversity and Second Language Learning.

McLaughlin, M. W., & Shepard, L. A. (1995). *Improving education through standards-based reform.* Stanford, CA: National Academy of Education.

National Association of Bilingual Education. (1992). *Professional standards for the preparation of bilingual/multicultural teachers.* Washington, DC: Author.

National Board for Professional Teaching Standards. (1989). *What teachers should know and be able to do.* Retrieved January 15, 2002, from http://www.nbpts.org/standards/

National Council of Teachers of English and International Reading Association. (1996). *Standards for the English language arts.* Urbana, IL, and Newark, DE: Author.

Pajares, M. (1992). Teachers' beliefs and educational research: Clearing up a messy construct. *Review of Educational Research, 62* (3), 307-332.

Ramirez, J. D., Yuen, S. D., & Ramey, D. R. (1991). *Longitudinal study of structured English immersion strategy, early-exit transitional bilingual education programs for language minority children. Final report* (vols. 1-2). San Mateo, CA: Aguirre International.

Richardson, V., Anders, P., Tidwell, D., & Lloyd, C. (1991). The relationship between teachers' beliefs and practices in reading comprehension instruction. *American Education Research Journal, 28,* 559-586.

Rueda, R. (1998). *Standards for professional development: A sociocultural perspective* (Research Brief No. 2). Washington, DC, and Santa Cruz, CA: Center for Research on Education, Diversity & Excellence.

Snow, C. E. (1987). Relevance of the notion of a critical period to language acquisition. In M. Bornstein (Ed.), *Sensitive periods in development* (pp. 183-209). Hillsdale, NJ: Erlbaum.

Standards for Teacher Education, Colorado Revised Statutes of 2000, § 23-1-121 (4)(d).

Teachers of English to Speakers of Other Languages. (1997). *ESL standards for pre-K–12 students.* Alexandria, VA: Author.

Tharp, R. (1997). *From at-risk to excellence: Research, theory, and principles for practice* (Research Rep. No. 1). Washington, DC, and Santa Cruz, CA: Center for Research on Education, Diversity & Excellence.

# Chapter Four

# Teacher Knowledge About Language

Virginia Richardson
University of Michigan

In responding to Fillmore & Snow's paper, I offer first the kind of reaction that many teacher educators experience when they confront yet another suggestion for an additional course or curriculum element. Then I respond to Fillmore and Snow's very serious endeavor to rethink the nature of the understandings teachers should have about language when entering the classroom.

In their chapter, Fillmore and Snow develop a compelling rationale for why teachers need to know more about language in their roles as communicator, educator, evaluator, educated human being, and agent of socialization. They then organize the knowledge base that teachers need according to 10 questions that teachers should be able to answer. While existing teacher education classes undoubtedly deal with some of this material, much of it may not be covered. The authors propose to distribute this knowledge across seven possible courses. These courses are meant to be taken within the pedagogical sequence, rather than within the general education or content elements of a teacher education program, or perhaps during inservice education.

Fillmore and Snow propose an enormous number of topics that teachers should know about. They do not stand alone in their call to add to the teacher education curriculum, however. There are constant attempts to add credit hours and topics to the already crowded and tightly structured preservice teacher education curriculum. New topics that have been proposed include, probably quite appropriately, women's studies, geography, a second course in student learning and development, urban education, rural education, and teaching profoundly handicapped individuals (in addition to an already-required special education course). An initial pragmatic response to such requests is, "Get in line." Preservice teacher education is faced with a limited number of credit hours within which to prepare teachers. These hours are often state-mandated both in number and in topic. Many programs require just 1 year (e.g., 5th-year Masters in Teaching programs), and few are longer than 2, with a considerable amount of time and credit hours consumed by student teaching. I assume that Fillmore and Snow are not suggesting that all seven courses they propose be taken during the preservice teacher preparation program. But adding just one course is a challenge—let alone subtracting one to add another.

I move now from the pragmatic critique to an examination of Fillmore and Snow's serious and deep analysis of the linguistic knowledge that teachers should possess in order to operate effectively in today's classrooms. I do not intend to question the nature of the formal knowledge they present or its representation in five teacher functions, ten questions, and seven courses. Others have taken up that challenge. Instead, I place Fillmore and Snow's work within a larger frame of knowledge that teachers acquire, develop, and use in their classrooms. I outline key conceptualizations of knowledge in order to raise questions concerning the depth of understanding about language that teachers need for their work and about how this understanding relates to teaching in the classroom. I also address the ways in which formal knowledge, such as the knowledge about language that Fillmore and Snow advocate, is held by teachers and used in teaching action. With this discussion as background, I refocus on the formal knowledge presented by Fillmore and Snow.

## Teacher Knowledge

In recent years, teacher knowledge has been of considerable interest in research on teaching and the focus of extensive debate. The research on teacher knowledge addresses such issues as the relationship among beliefs, knowledge, and action; forms of knowledge held by teachers; and how teach-ers learn to teach.[1] The debates address two issues: the definition of knowl-edge and whether it should be treated primarily as a philosophical or an experiential construct; and whether there is a difference between formal knowledge and practical knowledge. In the philosophically grounded litera-ture, a distinction is made between beliefs and knowledge. Knowledge depends on a warrant or justification that addresses the validity of a proposi-tion as understood within a community (Green, 1971; Lehrer, 1990). This def-inition of knowledge anchors the concept outside the domain of the individual. A belief, on the other hand, does not require a warrant. The body of understandings about language that Fillmore and Snow address is an exam-ple of this warranted and community-held notion of knowledge.

The experiential definition of knowledge, on the other hand, ignores the justification condition. For example, Alexander (2000) describes knowledge this way:

> **Broadly defined, knowledge signifies all that one knows or believes, without direct consideration of the source of that knowledge, its explicitness, or its veracity. . . . Knowledge from this epistemological vantage point constitutes the realm of human understanding, whether accurate or incomplete, declarative or procedural, tacit or explicit. (p. 29)**

This definition places knowledge solely within the individual as a major fac-tor that affects action.

The second debate focuses on the nature of formal and practical knowledge. From Aristotle to Fenstermacher (1979) and Schön (1983), an epistemologi-cal distinction has been drawn between practical knowledge and formal knowledge.[2] Practical knowledge is that which accrues from experience in practice; formal knowledge consists of those understandings that are war-ranted and accepted within a community. However, for those who operate within the strictly experiential conceptualization in which knowledge is all that does and can come to an individual's mind—even that which is not con-scious—such an epistemological differentiation between formal and practical knowledge is not possible. As Fenstermacher (1994) pointed out in his article on teacher knowing, experiential scholars use the term *knowledge* as a grouping term. For example, Alexander, Schallert, and Hare (1991) described 26 terms for knowledge that are used in the literature on literacy, terms that are not meant to be epistemologically distinct.

In addition to disagreement about the definition of knowledge, there are also socio-political concerns about the distinction between formal and practical knowledge. Critics suggest that such a differentiation automatically privileges formal over practical knowledge and thereby relegates teachers as practical knowledge producers to a lower status than researchers (see, for example, Anderson & Herr, 1999; Cochran-Smith & Lytle, 1999).

In my work as researcher and teacher educator, I find that the distinctions between knowledge and beliefs and between formal and practical knowledge are useful (Richardson, 1996). If one accepts all experienced understanding as knowledge, standards for veracity are difficult to employ: Knowledge, by definition, may include deception, illusion, and falsehood. Is there incorrect or untruthful knowledge? On the other hand, if one accepts a differentiation between beliefs and knowledge, beliefs may be examined in relation to knowledge that derives from research and scholarship on certain phenomena.[3] Thus in this chapter, I am using *knowledge* as a term that does not include beliefs and requires a warrant.

Differentiating formal and practical knowledge helps to explain the lack of clear and linear relationships between the theory and research-based knowledge of learning and teaching, on the one hand, and teaching actions on the other. It also helps explain the remarkable amount of often tacit understanding that appears to be a part of actions teachers take at particular moments within specific contexts. Since this book focuses on knowledge about language that needs to be acquired during teacher education, I use the epistemological distinction between formal and practical knowledge. I describe two forms of formal knowledge (disciplinary and foundational) that are not differentiated epistemologically but are appropriately grouped in two categories of the teacher education curriculum.

# Formal Knowledge

Formal knowledge consists of understandings that are agreed upon within a community of scholars as worthwhile and justified. Formal knowledge goes well beyond facts to include arguments, argument form, disciplinary structures and habits of mind, the intellectual history of a field, and the appropriate methodology for determining veracity. Within teacher education, formal knowledge may be divided into two forms that relate to the curriculum: discipline knowledge and foundational knowledge.

## Discipline Knowledge

This knowledge relates to the subject matter curriculum that teachers and students enact in the classroom. A teacher's disciplinary knowledge includes an understanding of the structure and logic of the discipline as well as its substance. By and large, preservice secondary education students are required to obtain a major or its equivalent in the subject that they are planning to teach and sometimes a minor in another discipline. Elementary preservice students are also often required to major in a subject, but this is not always the case because elementary teachers usually need to know about many subjects.

## Foundational Knowledge

This is knowledge that surrounds and influences the teaching act. It does not become a part of the formal preK–12 school curriculum but is used by teachers in enacting the curriculum, organizing and managing the classroom, interacting with students, and working collectively with other professionals within and outside school settings. Foundational knowledge includes such areas (and often courses) as general studies, student learning and development (educational psychology), educational foundations and policy, teachers and teaching, multicultural education, literacy across the curriculum, and special education. The knowledge field concerning language that Fillmore and Snow describe is one type of foundational knowledge.

Discipline and foundational knowledge sometimes come together in the scholarship on teaching. Shulman (1986), for example, posits a form of knowledge that combines disciplinary and foundational knowledge: *pedagogical content knowledge*, which involves teachers knowing their subject matter in a way that brings foundational knowledge about student learning and the classroom context together with subject matter knowledge to bear on instruction.

## Practical Knowledge

Practical knowledge is acquired through experience in teaching. First explored with regard to teaching by Elbaz (1983) and developed further by Clandinin and Connelly (1987), practical knowledge is often tacit and contextual. It is conceived of as embodied in the whole person, not just the mind; and it relates, in part, to the way people physically interact with the environment (Johnson, 1987). This knowledge is personalized, idiosyncratic, and contextual, and, for Yinger (1987), it emerges during action.

Practical knowledge is of particular importance to teaching because teaching involves action and is highly contextual. The issue of how to begin the acquisition of practical knowledge in preservice education, prior to the student's becoming a teacher, remains a challenge for teacher educators. The use of cases (J. Shulman, 1992), early practica in the field, simulations, and analysis of videotapes (Lampert & Ball, 1999) may help to introduce students to practical knowledge and bring formal knowledge and practice together. But the relationship between formal knowledge and practical knowledge remains unclear, as does the relationship between formal knowledge and classroom action.

Two issues arise in considering the formal knowledge covered in preservice teacher education. One, mentioned above, concerns the relationship between formal and practical knowledge and the relationship of both to teacher action. Since teaching is action,[4] it would be helpful to know how the various forms of knowledge are, or should be, used in the teaching act. The second issue pertains to how deeply preservice teacher education students should hold this knowledge. This consideration relates, in part, to how we think knowledge should be used or represented in the classroom.

# Relationships Among Forms of Knowledge and Teaching Action

Doyle (1979) suggests that the classroom is an ecological system with six properties that help to drive teaching action: multidimensionality, simultaneity, immediacy, unpredictability, publicness, and history. These properties affect the way in which teachers' knowledge and understandings are used in the classroom context. A surface analysis would suggest that the clearest relationship between teachers' formal knowledge and classroom action lies in discipline knowledge. After all, in order to teach history, teachers need to have formal knowledge of history. In fact, there is one view of teaching, developed by Stephens (1967) and described and critiqued by Murray (1996), that suggests that teachers simply require subject matter knowledge in combination with a set of natural human tendencies, such as the tendency to talk about what one knows. Hiring teachers would involve assessing their subject matter understanding and their innate natural teaching tendencies. This sense of natural teaching still prevails in the many calls for reform in teacher education that emphasize courses in the disciplinary majors with a concomitant reduced emphasis on pedagogical education.

However, while content knowledge is clearly important in classroom action, the relationship with formal knowledge is not linear. Representing disciplinary knowledge in the classroom requires much more than simply understanding that knowledge (Grossman, 1990; L. S. Shulman, 1986): It requires pedagogical content knowledge.

The relationship between foundational knowledge and teaching action is even more of a puzzle. At what point, and how, will teachers use their formal understanding of school finance, student efficacy theory, or "the wide array of writing systems that exist in the world's languages" (Fillmore & Snow, this volume, p.34) in their classroom actions? Not only do we not know the answer to this question empirically, we often do not have normative expectations for such use. I am certainly not suggesting that this knowledge is not used by teachers in their classrooms. My sense is that much of the foundational knowledge contributes to teachers' approaches to knowledge and teaching, habits of mind, views of themselves as professionals, understandings of and ability to determine what students bring with them to the classroom, and understandings of the connection between their classrooms and the larger society in making ethical decisions for their students in light of the society's democratic ideals. And much of this knowledge may eventually be internalized and folded within practical knowledge.

Some of the formal foundational knowledge that teachers learn may be somewhat linearly related to classroom action, such as the theory and practice of specific classroom strategies like cooperative learning. Normative expectations are made explicit when the teacher educator introduces cooperative learning to the students: That is, cooperative learning is a good approach to use in a heterogeneous classroom when you want students to cooperate on learning a topic in the curriculum or completing a jointly produced project.

I mentioned above that foundational knowledge may be folded within practical knowledge. At this point in the research that focuses on teacher cognition, the relationship between formal knowledge and practical knowledge is extremely unclear. Fenstermacher and I have developed and studied a way of bringing formal knowledge into teachers' reflections and everyday teacher actions (Fenstermacher, 1994; Fenstermacher & Richardson, 1993). Calling it the Practical Argument Process, we work with individual teachers in examining videotapes of their teaching to elicit their premises for practice and explore alternative premises derived from recent research and theory. This strategy is viewed as a change process rather than a descriptive study of the ways in which formal knowledge becomes translated into or embedded within practical knowledge and action.

## Depth of Knowledge

A second issue concerns the depth at which teacher education students should hold formal knowledge so that it becomes useful in teaching. I could, for example, give my M.A. certification students a paper on some aspect of language use and tell them that there will be a quiz on it. The students would be able to do very well on a multiple-choice test concerning the information in that document. Would this mean that they now know what teachers need to know about language use? Perhaps something about it. But if knowledge were retained at all, it would be held in a form that probably would not be particularly useful in the classroom. To be of use in action, a depth of understanding is required for use in planning, instructional action, student assessment, and reflection. In order for foundational knowledge to be helpful in teaching practice, it needs to be so deeply held by teachers that it may be used in determining and interpreting the meanings that their students bring to the classroom. This requirement speaks to the dilemma of depth versus breadth in content coverage that is faced by all teachers and teacher educators.

## An Example of Knowledge Use in Teacher Education

I present now an example of knowledge development and use involving my own attempts at helping teacher education students gain an understanding of culture that they could eventually use in classroom teaching. My point concerns the depth of understanding that is required to make sense of and use such knowledge in a teacher education classroom: It took considerable time for me to acquire this understanding, and it takes time for teacher education students to acquire it as well. And yet knowledge of cultural differences is just one among many elements suggested by Fillmore and Snow.

My memory of this incident was triggered by a description in the Fillmore/Snow chapter of cultural differences in the concept of self in relation to family and community. They suggest that Mexican children "have a sure sense of self within the world of the home" (Fillmore & Snow, this volume, p. 18). Then they refer to Popovi Da (1969) for a description of Pueblo Indian children: "The central unit is the community, and its needs and requirements take precedence over those of the individual" (Fillmore & Snow, this volume, p. 18). They go on to suggest that teachers should be cognizant of these differences.

When I moved to the University of Arizona as a teacher educator, I read a number of books and articles to prepare myself both to understand my students and to prepare them for cultural diversity in the classroom (e.g., Au & Jordan, 1981; Greenbaum & Greenbaum, 1981; Philips, 1983; and, later, a novel by Barbara Kingsolver, 1993). This foundational knowledge suggested to me that the world view of the American Indian child was very different from that of the Anglo child, at least in terms of identity as a community member and as an individual. I found this to be a profoundly difficult difference to appreciate. This was not merely an issue of competitive versus cooperative groups. These are Anglo terms developed within an individualistic culture. My Anglo world is so deeply individualistic that developing an intense or even modest understanding of what it would mean to have a community-oriented identity was extraordinarily difficult. From assessment practices to playing sports, obtaining a job, and respecting individual rights, this is an individualistic society.

I worked hard at making sense of such differences, and I still do. I also worked with my teacher education students on these concepts and was helped myself by the diversity within these classes. I believed that understanding these world view differences is extremely important to teachers in the Southwest. Nonetheless, just as I had difficulty placing myself within the community-oriented paradigm, so too did my Anglo students. They certainly could have passed a multiple choice test after I addressed the subject the first time. But that form of knowing would have been of little help to them as they entered the world of classroom action. As mentioned above, it is best that this formal foundational knowledge be deeply held, if not internalized, such that it can affect classroom action in many different ways.

But even more difficult to contemplate is how this knowledge *should* be used in classroom action. Some of the research on cultural differences is immediately useful. For example, "Don't form negative views about your students when they don't look you in the eye" is an easy notion to get across and to remember. If my students were to end up teaching on Indian reservations, knowledge about identity would be helpful in organizing tasks that did not rely on competition among individuals. The teacher might begin to slowly introduce students to the nature of a competitive society, were the community interested in preparing students for non-reservation life. However, many of my teacher education students ended up teaching in classrooms with diverse populations of students: Anglo, Hispanic, American Indian, and African American.

The best that I could do as a teacher educator was to help the students develop a tolerance for diversity and understand that differences in how children approach tasks may be related to cultural background. At the same time, it was important to stress that teachers should not stereotype on the basis of cultural background. The question of what learning tasks to select in either a homogeneous or heterogeneous classroom remains open. The responses to such questions rely on more than knowledge of language and culture. These become deeply ethical issues that must be worked out by the teacher within the specific community context in which the school is located, as well as in consideration of school district goals, state standards, and national ideals.

## Knowledge of Language in the Teacher Education Curriculum

The type of knowledge about language that Fillmore and Snow endorse in their chapter is formal and foundational in nature, and questions may be asked about all such knowledge. A first set of questions relates to the depth of understanding of the language curriculum that the authors are proposing for teacher education students. Within this set are questions about the pragmatics of when and how this knowledge should be introduced. A second set of questions relates to the relationship between this knowledge and teacher action in the classroom.

An enormous amount of information is presented to preservice teacher education students. Not only are they learning their subject matter disciplines, they are also being introduced to a number of additional disciplines that relate to learning, teaching, and schooling: psychology, history, philosophy, sociology, anthropology, and linguistics, among others. Obviously not all of this knowledge can be internalized in the very short period of time that students are studying teaching prior to becoming teachers. Fillmore and Snow are presenting the linguistics case and suggesting that the material could be covered in seven courses. This can't happen in the preservice curriculum at this point. Is it possible to focus on a subset of this material without losing its disciplinary character? Are there important themes that we want preservice students to walk away with? Can they learn this material after they start teaching?

The second set of questions relates to the relationship between formal and practical knowledge and between these forms of knowledge and classroom action. In other words, is the knowledge covered in preservice teacher education worthwhile? Disciplinary knowledge is extremely important; one would think that knowledge of how children develop and learn, how various systems affect schools and classrooms, and how language is structured are important as well. Questions of practice, though, seldom map on to questions asked by scholars within a field. In response to the instantaneous demands of the classroom, foundational knowledge in a particular area has to be quickly melded with knowledge in other areas and knowledge of the classroom context, resulting in action that may be difficult to trace to a specific foundational area. Perhaps what we can hope for is that teachers reflect on classroom questions and dilemmas using constructs that are helpful in the immediate context— but more importantly, that teachers continue to pursue foundational knowledge that provides some clarification to their questions and points toward potential changes in practice. We would also hope that teachers are able to explore and justify their classroom actions with premises drawn from formal and practical knowledge.

Three possible approaches in preservice teacher education may deal with the problem of the massive curriculum: 1) Cover as much content as possible during preservice teacher education so that some of these constructs may stick, to be called upon in times of need; 2) within the teacher education program, develop a set of themes that are close to practice and that cut across many foundational areas; 3) recognize that preservice teacher education students can't possibly retain this knowledge for long and consider developing programs of staff development in which foundational knowledge may be used to question, explain, justify, and develop practical knowledge.[5]

At this point, I engage in all three of these approaches, but I believe that we ought to consider the theme approach more fully than we have in preservice teacher education. Done well, a theme such as culture and cultural differences, described in relation to language in the Fillmore/Snow chapter, would eventually allow teachers to focus on problems of practice and understand how a response to these problems can be informed by foundational understandings. This approach would bring together formal and practical knowledge. Issues of culture and cultural difference should be addressed in all foundational classes with an emphasis on how a particular foundational understanding can contribute to an understanding of these issues and toward possible action plans. In addition, because many of the teacher action decisions that are surrounded by formal knowledge of language and culture are also ethical in nature, students should have the opportunity to understand the ethical dilemmas they may face in the diverse classroom as they are presented with formal knowledge about language and culture.

# Notes

¹ For thorough reviews of the literature, see Borko & Putnam (1996), Carter (1990), Fenstermacher (1994), Munby, Martin, & Russell (in press), and Richardson (1996).

² From an epistemological point of view, both formal and practical knowledge require justification or warrant, although "they are different undertakings depending on the domain in which one states one's claims. What distinguishes this effort in the practical as opposed to the formal domain is that we do not require the methods or other paraphernalia of science" (Fenstermacher, 1994, p. 28).

³ At the same time, I am aware that our knowledge base shifts as we move through time and continual exploration of empirical premises.

⁴ I use the term *action* rather than *behavior* because action combines behaviors with intentions. According to David (1994), "1) Actions are doings having mentalistic explanations of a certain sort. 2) Actions are doings that are intentional under some descriptions. 3) Actions are doings that begin with a certain kind of event. 4) Actions are doings of which the doer has a certain kind of awareness" (p. 112). David asserts that actions are one or any combination of the above.

⁵ Fenstermacher (1993) has suggested that teacher education students should begin to develop practical knowledge as soon as they enter the program through internships in the field. After several years of a mentoring apprenticeship approach, they should then return to the university for topics in foundations, psychology, pedagogical content knowledge, and so forth. (See also Tom, 1995.)

# References

Alexander, P. (2000). Toward a model of academic development: Schooling and the acquisition of knowledge. *Educational Researcher, 29*(2), 28-33.

Alexander, P. A., Schallert, D. L., & Hare, V. (1991). Coming to terms: How researchers in learning and literacy talk about knowledge. *Review of Educational Research, 61*(3), 315-343.

Anderson G. L., & Herr, K. (1999). The new paradigm wars: Is there room for rigorous practitioner knowledge in schools and universities? *Educational Researcher, 28*(5), 12-21.

Au, K., & Jordan, C. (1981). Teaching reading to Hawaiian children. In H. Trueba, G. Guthrie, & K. Au (Eds.), *Culture and the bilingual classroom* (pp. 139-152). Rowley, MA: Newbury.

Borko, H., & Putnam, R. (1996). Learning to teach. In R. C. Calfee & D. C. Berliner (Eds.), *Handbook of educational psychology* (pp. 673-708). New York: Macmillan.

Carter, K. (1990). Teachers' knowledge and learning to teach. In W. R. Houston (Ed.), *Handbook of research on teacher education* (pp. 291-310). New York: Macmillan.

Clandinin, D. J., & Connelly, F. M. (1987). Teachers' personal knowledge: What counts as personal in studies of the personal. *Journal of Curriculum Studies, 19*(6), 487-500.

Cochran-Smith, M., & Lytle, S. L. (1999). The teacher research movement: A decade later. *Educational Researcher, 28*(7), 15-25.

David, L. H. (1994) Action (1). In S. Guttenplan (Ed.), *A companion to the philosophy of mind* (pp. 111-117). London: Blackwell.

Doyle, W. (1979). Classroom tasks and students' abilities. In P. L. Peterson & H. J. Walberg (Eds.), *Research on teaching: Concepts, findings and implications* (pp. 183–209). Berkeley, CA: McCutchan.

Elbaz, F. L. (1983). *Teacher thinking: A study of practical knowledge.* London: Croom Helm.

Fenstermacher, G. D. (1979). A philosophical consideration of recent research on teacher effectiveness. In L. S. Shulman (Ed.), *Review of research in education* (vol. 6, pp. 157–185). Itasca, IL: Peacock.

Fenstermacher, G. D. (1993). *Where are we going? Who will lead us there?* Washington, DC: American Association of Colleges of Teacher Education.

Fenstermacher, G. D. (1994). The knower and the known: The nature of knowledge in research on teaching. In L. Darling-Hammond (Ed.), *Review of research in education* (vol. 20, pp. 1–54). Washington: American Educational Research Association.

Fenstermacher, G. D., & Richardson, V. (1993). The elicitation and reconstruction of practical arguments in teaching. *Journal of Curriculum Studies, 25*(2), 101–114.

Green, T. (1971). *The activities of teaching.* New York: McGraw-Hill.

Greenbaum, P. E., & Greenbaum, S. D. (1981). Cultural differences, nonverbal regulation, and classroom interaction: Sociolinguistic interference in American Indian education. *Peabody Journal of Education, 61*(1), 16–33.

Grossman, P. (1990). *The making of a teacher: Teacher knowledge and teacher education.* New York: Teachers College Press.

Johnson, M. (1987). *The body in the mind: The bodily basis of meaning, imagination, and mind.* Chicago: University of Chicago Press.

Kingsolver, B. (1993). *Pigs in heaven*. New York: HarperCollins.

Lampert, M., & Ball, D. (1999). *Investigating teaching: New pedagogies and new technologies for teacher education*. Teachers College Press.

Lehrer, K. (1990). *Theory of knowledge*. Boulder, CO: Westview Press.

Munby, H., Martin, A., & Russell, T. (in press). In V. Richardson (Ed.). *Handbook of research on teaching* (4th ed.). Washington, DC: American Educational Research Association.

Murray, F. (1996). Beyond natural teaching: The case for professional education. In F. Murray (Ed.), *The teacher educator's handbook: Building a knowledge base for the preparation of teachers* (pp. 3-13). San Francisco: Jossey-Bass.

Philips, S. (1983). *The invisible culture*. New York: Longman.

Popovi Da. (1969). Indian values. *Journal of the Southwest Association of Indian Affairs*, 15-19.

Richardson, V. (1996). Conducting research on teacher education. In F. Murray (Ed.), *Handbook for teacher educators* (pp. 715-737). San Francisco: Jossey-Bass.

Schön, D. A. (1983). *The reflective practitioner*. New York: Basic Books.

Shulman, J. (Ed.). (1992). *Case methods in teacher education*. New York: Teachers College Press.

Shulman, L. S. (1986). Those who understand: Knowledge growth in teaching. *Educational Researcher, 15*(7), 4-14.

Stephens, J. M. (1967). *The process of schooling: A psychological examination*. Austin, TX: Holt, Rinehart & Winston.

Tom, A. (1995). Stirring the embers: Reconsidering the structure of teacher education programs. In M. Wideen & P. Grimmett (Eds.), *Changing times in teacher education* (pp. 117–132). London: Falmer.

Yinger, R. (1987, April). *By the seat of your pants: An inquiry into improvisation in teaching.* Paper presented at the annual meeting of the American Educational Research Association, Washington, DC.

## Chapter Five

# Incorporating Linguistic Knowledge in Standards for Teacher Performance

Donna M. Gollnick
National Council for Accreditation of Teacher Education

In asserting that teachers need to have a much better understanding of language to help their students develop language skills,[1] Fillmore and Snow point to the increasing number of children of immigrants in the nation's classrooms, as well as students who speak regional and cultural dialects that are different from those of mainstream America. These students continue to challenge educators' knowledge and beliefs about language, despite accumulating research on patterns in English language learning (Hakuta, Butler, & Witt, 2000) and on the structure of American English (Wolfram & Schilling-Estes, 1998). Too often these students are labeled by schools as not academically able. Such labels, which are based on unwarranted assumptions about language, limit students' potential for success in school and in the workforce.

To a great extent, academic and career success is dependent on the use of Standard English in education and work settings. In preparing students for this linguistic reality, school practice has often focused on eliminating other languages and vernacular dialects rather than adding to them (Brisk, 1998). Being fluent in multiple languages and dialects is not valued in the United States unless one's first language is English and one's first dialect is Standard English. Students may forget their first languages over time as schools focus on teaching them the one way to speak and write that can help move them into the middle class and into professional-level jobs. As a result, many immigrant students cannot communicate effectively with parents and grandparents who have little, if any, English proficiency.

But there are more effective ways for schools to approach language differences. Standard English can and should be taught to all students without denigrating the native languages and dialects of their families (Wolfram, Adger, & Christian, 1999). Students should be encouraged to speak and write two or more languages fluently. And rather than eliminating their regional or cultural dialects, students should become adept at using them along with Standard English to negotiate effectively in the range of social settings they encounter.

For decades, multicultural and bilingual educators have been promoting policies and programs that support the development of Standard English while using students' native languages and dialects in the classroom. The accrediting agency for the preparation of teachers and other school personnel, the National Council for Accreditation of Teacher Education (NCATE), has required for 25 years that its accredited institutions prepare school personnel to work effectively with students from diverse ethnic, racial, language, socioeconomic, gender, religious, and regional backgrounds as well as with students with exceptionalities. In this chapter, I assume that these requirements are being met, and I react primarily to Fillmore and Snow's recommendations for additional teacher preparation in literacy and language learning.

## Options for Accommodating Educational Linguistics

Most teacher education programs do not have room in the curriculum to add to the coursework now in place (Baca & Escamilla, this volume; Richardson, this volume). Many state legislatures or boards of education have limited the number of credit hours that can be offered in the education component of a teacher education program to allow more time in subject matter preparation (Baca & Escamilla, this volume). Most candidates in secondary teaching programs major in the subject that they plan to teach and minor in a related area. Candidates in elementary education and special education usually take more coursework in education than their secondary education counterparts, but sometimes they are required to major in a field other than education. A number of state agencies have limited the hours required for a baccalaureate to approximately 120. This constraint has led to rigidly prescribed offerings for teacher candidates who must major and minor in an academic area and also complete professional requirements for teaching. There may be no time left to develop the knowledge and skills recommended by Fillmore and Snow.

Several options do exist for solving the packed-curriculum problem, however. Perhaps the current coursework and practical experiences required for professional teacher preparation are no longer appropriate. Education faculty should periodically review and revise the requirements. They might follow the lead of NCATE, state agencies, and national professional associations as they move from a system of specific curricular requirements to one that details expectations for candidate performance. If education faculty determined the knowledge, skills, and dispositions that beginning teachers should possess by the time they finish a teacher education program, the curriculum might evolve in a direction that is quite different from today's.

NCATE has developed six standards for teacher candidates, three of which focus on candidate performance and ability to teach all students:

- Candidates[2] preparing to work in schools as teachers or other professional school personnel know and demonstrate the content, pedagogical, and professional knowledge, skills, and dispositions necessary to help all students[3] learn. Assessments indicate that candidates meet professional, state, and institutional[4] standards. (Standard 1 on Candidate Knowledge, Skills, and Dispositions)
- The unit[5] and its school partners design, implement, and evaluate field experiences and clinical practice so that teacher candidates and other school personnel develop and demonstrate the knowledge, skills, and dispositions necessary to help all students learn. (Standard 3 on Field Experiences and Clinical Practice)
- The unit designs, implements, and evaluates curriculum and experiences for candidates to acquire and apply the knowledge, skills, and dispositions necessary to help all students learn. These experiences include working with diverse higher education and school faculty, diverse candidates, and diverse students in preK–12 schools. (Standard 4 on Diversity) (National Council for Accreditation of Teacher Education, 2002, p. 10)

| Fillmore & Snow | Elementary Education (NCATE and the Association for Childhood Education International, 2000) | English Language Arts (National Council of Teachers of English, 1996) | Reading Specialists (International Reading Association, 1998) |
|---|---|---|---|
| Language and Linguistics | Candidates<br><br>• are adept at teaching the fundamentals of the English language arts. They model effective use of English, including its syntax, lexicon, history, varieties, literature, and oral and written composing processes.<br><br>• know what preconceptions, error patterns, and misconceptions they may expect to find in students' understanding of how language functions in communication, and they are able to help students correct their misunderstandings of the development and uses of language. *(from Supporting Explanation)* | [The candidate will]<br><br>• show an understanding of the evolution of the English language and the historical influences on its various forms.<br><br>• demonstrate an understanding of English grammar.<br><br>• demonstrate an understanding of semantics, syntax, morphology, and phonology. | |
| Language and Cultural Diversity | Candidates understand how elementary students differ in their development and approaches to learning and create instructional opportunities that are adapted to diverse students. *(Standard 3b)* | [The candidate will]<br><br>• use the English language arts to help students become familiar with their own and others' cultures.<br><br>• recognize the impact that culture, societal events and issues have on teachers, students, the English language arts curriculum, and education in general.<br><br>• recognize the impact of cultural, economic, political, and social environments upon language.<br><br>• show a respect for and an understanding of diversity in language use, patterns, and dialects across cultures, ethnic groups, geographic regions, and social roles.<br><br>• show knowledge of a broad historical and contemporary spectrum of United States, British, and world literatures, including works from a | [The reading professional will]<br><br>• demonstrate an understanding and respect for cultural, linguistic, and ethnic diversity in the teaching process.<br><br>• demonstrate an understanding of the impact of . . . cultural . . . factors on learning, language evelopment, and reading acquisition. |

Table 1    Comparison of Professional Association Standards and Fillmore and Snow's Recommendations

| | | | |
|---|---|---|---|
| Sociolinguistics for Educators in a Linguistically Diverse Society | | ...respect for and support of individual differences of ethnicity, race, language, culture, gender, and ability. | |
| Language Development | [Candidates] use their knowledge and understanding of language, first and second language development, and the language arts to design instructional programs and strategies that build on students' experiences and existing language skills and result in their students becoming competent, effective users of language. *(from Supporting Explanation)* | [The candidate will] • show an understanding of language acquisition and development. • demonstrate how reading, writing, speaking, listening, viewing, and thinking are interrelated. | [The reading professional will] demonstrate an understanding of • the major theories of language development, cognition, and learning. • the interrelation of language and literacy acquisition. • phonemic, morphemic, semantic, syntactic, and pragmatic systems of language and their relation to the reading and writing process. |
| Second Language Learning and Teaching | See language development above. | | |
| The Language of Academic Discourse | | | [The reading professional will] • ensure that students gain understanding of the meaning and importance of the conventions of standard written English (e.g., punctuation or usage). • teach students the conventions of standard written English needed to edit their compositions. |
| Text Analysis and Language Understanding in Educational Settings | | | |

In addition to a thorough overhaul of the curriculum, another option is to extend the time required to prepare teachers beyond the baccalaureate degree to allow for more in-depth study and practice as is required in a number of other professional fields. Some institutions have developed 5-year programs that end with a master's degree or post-baccalaureate licensure. Others prepare teachers only at the master's level with 1 year of concentrated study, often including an internship that extends beyond one semester. Both of these options allow candidates to major and minor in an academic discipline, yet have additional time to focus on the knowledge essential for teaching and learning and to develop the skills and dispositions for helping all students learn. It must be noted, however, that even though these programs include more time for learning overall, they probably do not attend to the issues of culture and linguistics in education that are raised by Fillmore and Snow.

The recommendations of these authors may be more critical to the preparation of elementary school teachers, teachers in bilingual education, teachers of English as a second language, reading teachers, and English language arts teachers than to teachers in other areas. In fact, there is a precedent for addressing much of the language knowledge that Fillmore and Snow advocate for teacher education. The national standards for the preparation of teachers in these fields include some of the critical areas they recommend, as shown in Table 1. (For this table, I have drawn on the standards approved by NCATE.[6] The professional organization for Teachers of English to Speakers of Other Languages (TESOL) developed standards that were approved by NCATE in October 2001. Standards for the preparation of bilingual education teachers have not been presented to NCATE.

## Confronting Limitations

Table 1 reveals contrasts among the professional standards for teachers of English language arts and those for reading teachers and the categories of language knowledge that Fillmore and Snow propose. Even the specialists who have primary responsibility for teaching students to read, write, and speak are not expected by their professional associations to develop knowledge and skills related to linguistic analysis, sociolinguistics, second language learning, and text analysis for instructional purposes. This discrepancy has consequences for students' learning. The students who will suffer the most from inattention to these areas are those who come to school as English language learners or with a regional or cultural dialect that contrasts with the school's expectations. Fillmore and Snow point out that students who enter school speaking little or no English have not been receiving the instruction they require to master English language structures and patterns of use. If professional standards function as limits on the teacher preparation curriculum, this situation may not be remedied.

NCATE and most professional associations expect all teachers to understand diversity and be able to build on students' cultural and language backgrounds to help them learn. In the past, accreditation teams looked for evidence that the curriculum covered diversity topics, but they did not look for evidence that teacher candidates actually had developed the necessary knowledge bases and skills. Under the new NCATE standards, Board of Examiners teams will be looking for performance evidence that candidates are able to teach all students. Although language is included in NCATE's broad definition of *diversity* and *all students*, neither the standards nor their accompanying rubrics refer explicitly to English language learners. Candidates may complete teacher education programs with limited understanding of the complexity of language and language learning. They may not know that it takes students years to learn English well enough to handle academic tasks effectively, even though they are able to use English conversationally. They may not "know enough about language learning and language itself to evaluate the appropriateness of various methods, materials, and approaches for helping students make progress in learning English" (Fillmore & Snow, this volume, p. 33).

Despite the consequences of limited teacher knowledge about language and language learning, it may be that Fillmore and Snow are simply too optimistic in expecting all teachers to have the knowledge and skills outlined in their chapter. Nonetheless, it does seem appropriate for all teachers to have some basic understanding of (1) language and linguistics, (2) language and diversity, (3) sociolinguistics in a linguistically diverse society, (4) second language learning and teaching, which could include text analysis, and (5) the language of academic discourse. These knowledge bases and skills do not have to be translated into discrete courses in a teacher education program, but they should be incorporated into the curriculum, experiences, and assessments used throughout the program. Perhaps some of the knowledge related to language, linguistics, and diversity should be gained and enhanced through courses and experiences in arts and sciences prior to embarking on preparation for an education career. If teacher educators believe that these knowledge bases and skills are important, some of them should be assessed at admission into teacher education, others at completion of the program.

Teacher knowledge of language use patterns and language development processes is critical to ensuring that all children and youth have the opportunity to be academically successful. The chances that English language learners and students with stigmatized regional or cultural dialects will be left behind are great unless educators understand language, linguistics, cultural differences, and second language learning well enough to develop appropriate instructional strategies to help these students learn. How can we afford to place teachers in our classrooms who do not appreciate language diversity and who do not know how to help students understand and use English at a level necessary for academic discourse? If we are unwilling to take on the challenge of preparing teachers to work effectively with English language learners and students with stigmatized dialects, we will be failing both our children and our profession.

# Notes

[1] Although neither English language arts nor literacy are fields in which I am academically well grounded, I know that the authors are quite correct. The perspective offered here comes from my background in multicultural education and from NCATE's work in accreditation for teachers. It is influenced also by the fact that I did learn to diagram sentences in the third or fourth grade in a small rural school in Indiana. In addition, I was required to take a 1-hour speech course when I began college to unlearn my southern Indiana dialect.

[2] Candidates include persons preparing to teach; teachers who are continuing their professional development; and persons preparing for other professional roles in schools, such as principals, school psychologists, and school library media specialists.

[3] "All students" includes students with exceptionalities and of different ethnic, racial, gender, language, religious, socioeconomic, and regional/geographic origins.

[4] Institutional standards are reflected in the unit's conceptual framework and include candidate proficiencies.

[5] The unit is the institution, college, school, department, or other administrative body with the responsibility for managing or coordinating all programs offered for the initial and continuing preparation of teachers and other school personnel, regardless of where these programs are administratively housed.

[6] NCATE's program standards can be downloaded from its Web site at www.ncate.org.

# References

Brisk, M. E. (1998). *Bilingual education: From compensatory to quality schooling.* Mahwah, NJ: Erlbaum.

Hakuta, K., Butler, Y. G., & Witt, D. (2000). *How long does it take English learners to attain proficiency?* (Policy Report 2000-2001). Stanford: University of California Linguistic Minority Research Institute. Retrieved May 1, 2002, from http://www.stanford.edu/~hakuta/Docs/howLong.pdf

International Reading Association. (1998). *Standards for reading professionals* (Rev. ed.). Newark, DE: Author

National Council for Accreditation of Teacher Education. (2002). *Professional standards for the accreditation of schools, colleges, and departments of education.* Retrieved April 16, 2002, from http://www.ncate.org/2002/unit_stnds_2002.pdf

National Council for Accreditation of Teacher Education and Association for Childhood Education International. (2000). *Program standards for elementary teacher preparation.* Retrieved August 1, 2002, from http://www.udel.edu/bateman/acei/ncateindex.htm

National Council of Teachers of English. (1996). *Guidelines for the preparation of teachers of English language arts.* Urbana, IL: Author.

Wolfram, W., Adger, C. T., & Christian, D. (1999). *Dialects in schools and communities.* Mahwah, NJ: Erlbaum.

Wolfram, W., & Schilling-Estes, N. (1998). *American English: Dialects and variation.* Malden, MA: Blackwell.

# Chapter Six

# Preparing Teachers to Guide Children's Language Development

Sandra Feldman
American Federation of Teachers

Lily Wong Fillmore and Catherine Snow are absolutely right when they assert that it is necessary for teachers to systematically learn more about language if they are to successfully teach all children to read, write, and speak Standard English. They are also correct in asserting that teachers should acquire linguistic knowledge in the context of learning how language figures in education. The writers are not calling for making every teacher a linguist or a cultural anthropologist, but rather for including educational linguistics in the essential core of teachers' knowledge.

Teachers need to understand how central children's language is to who they are and how they define themselves. Teachers need to understand that children's language development involves acquiring not only the structure of the native language(s) but also fundamental patterns of social interaction. Virtually all children naturally develop the ability to use a language with complex rules that are consistent and that are shared by other members of their community. This apparently simple truth is perhaps the most important linguistic understanding for all teachers in our schools. Teachers must respect the language that children bring to school even as they teach them Standard English.

A critical role of the public school is to assure that all students, regardless of home language, master the language of the mainstream. They must have command of its conventions for speaking and writing. If children come to school speaking vernacular dialects or a language other than English, it is particularly important that they be taught Standard English directly. In such cases, what the teacher knows about language will greatly influence her success in helping students master Standard English and learn to read. Indeed, a good deal of the content of educational linguistics outlined by Fillmore and Snow is essential if we are to develop teachers who are able to be successful in our pluralistic classrooms, where demand for the skills and knowledge necessary for teaching Standard English grows more acute as school populations become ever more diverse.

Educational linguistics provides the substance for a serious course of study regarding multicultural pedagogy. A teacher who has mastered that curriculum will be a genuine multicultural educator whose pedagogy is culturally responsive and capitalizes on students' cultural backgrounds rather than overriding or negating them.

## The AFT Perspective on Literacy Instruction

The American Federation of Teachers (AFT) has long recognized the need for teachers to be better prepared if they are to meet the challenges of educating all of America's children to high standards (American Federation of Teachers, 2000a). We know that if teachers are expected to raise student achievement in a highly heterogeneous classroom, they need to acquire and continuously hone the skills necessary to do so. Teachers need to learn how difficult it can be for children to adapt to the culture, language, activities, manners, and ideologies promoted and experienced in school. They need knowledge that goes well beyond the popular diversity or multicultural sensitivity workshops currently offered to education professionals. When teachers have substantial knowledge about the structure of language, sociolinguistics, language development, and second language learning, they have the tools for helping children develop the language and literacy skills they need, and they have the mindset necessary to deal with unexpected turns in the path toward that goal.

The standards movement calls for different practices in teacher preparation and professionalism with regard to language and literacy. At present, many teachers are unprepared to teach to standards and to function effectively in linguistically, racially, culturally, and ethnically diverse classrooms. One result of this lack of appropriate preparation is the current high rate of reading difficulty, particularly among poor and minority children.

In many urban schools, student achievement is improving (American Federation of Teachers, 2000b), but it is nonetheless disturbing to find statistics that indicate that

- approximately 20% of elementary school students nationwide have significant problems learning to read.
- between 60% and 70% of English language learners and Latino and African American children have significant reading difficulties.
- at least 20% of elementary school students do not read fluently enough to enjoy or engage in independent reading.
- one third of poor readers nationwide are from college-educated families.
- 25% of adults lack the basic literacy skills required in a typical job. (American Federation of Teachers, 1999a, 1999b; Learning First Alliance & American Federation of Teachers, 1998)

These outcomes are unacceptable. Teachers must be better prepared to teach reading. The AFT has called for reform of teacher preparation and professional development to ensure that teachers know how to teach reading to all children, most particularly to English language learners and vernacular English speakers. As we noted in the preface to a recent publication,

> Reading is the fundamental skill upon which all formal education depends. Research now shows that a child who doesn't learn the reading basics early is unlikely to learn them at all. Any child who doesn't learn to read early and well will not master other skills and knowledge, and is unlikely to ever flourish in school or in life.
>
> Low reading achievement, more than any other factor, is the root cause of chronically low-performing schools, which harm

students and contribute to the loss of public confidence in our school system. When many children don't learn to read, the public schools cannot and will not be regarded as successful--and efforts to dismantle them will proceed. (American Federation of Teachers, 1999b, p. 5)

The AFT strongly believes that teachers in the primary grades, especially those who are given the responsibility of teaching reading, must be provided with expert training in reading pedagogy if they are to be held accountable for student achievement. Unlike acquiring spoken language, learning to read is not a process that occurs naturally. Reading must be learned through instruction.

A teacher who is well prepared to teach reading knows how to instruct students to decipher words in print, develop comprehension skills, and learn from text so that they enjoy reading. To be competent in reading instruction, a teacher must, at a minimum, have knowledge of the psychology of reading and its development; understand the structure of the English language; apply best practices in all aspects of reading instruction; and use validated, reliable, efficient assessments to inform classroom practice.

Studies have demonstrated that when teachers are adequately trained in reading pedagogy and have in-depth knowledge of language development and use, their students' achievement improves dramatically (August & Hakuta, 1997; Snow, Burns, & Griffin, 1998). But most teachers have at best a single reading methods course in their pre-service preparation, and the content of that course may not reflect the current consensus on reading instruction. Without a better understanding of the reading process and how students learn to read, teachers cannot adequately deliver reading instruction, nor can they properly assess reading performance, address student errors, anticipate the needs of slow and fast learners, or choose texts.

The AFT has proposed a core curriculum for teachers that dovetails with much of the linguistic knowledge that Fillmore and Snow believe to be essential (AFT, 1999b). We call for teachers to be educated to provide the following components and practices in their reading instruction:

- Direct teaching of decoding, comprehension, and literature appreciation.
- Phoneme awareness instruction.

- Systematic and explicit instruction in the code system of written English.
- Daily exposure to a variety of texts, as well as incentives for children to read independently and with others.
- Vocabulary instruction that includes a variety of complementary methods designed to explore the relationship among word structure, origin, and meaning.
- Comprehension strategies that include prediction of outcomes, summarizing, clarification, questioning, and visualization.
- Frequent writing of prose to enable deeper understanding of what is read.

## Getting the Job Done

Although there is research consensus on the knowledge teachers must master in order to develop student competence in language and literacy (Burns, Griffin, & Snow, 1998; National Reading Panel, 2000), many teachers have not had an opportunity to acquire that knowledge. We can no longer remain idle as large numbers of children fail to learn to read and are diagnosed incorrectly and disproportionately as having learning disabilities or mental retardation. University faculty must grant educational linguistics the importance it deserves, and in-service professional development must expose teachers to the consensus literature on how best to teach reading.

But this is more easily said than done. There are barriers that we must understand and overcome if we are to succeed in getting better pre-service preparation and in-service professional development for teachers:

- Most teacher education departments do not have faculty who can teach the prescribed content. Nor do most of them have access to faculty in the arts and sciences who are interested in developing such courses for teachers. It is necessary, as Fillmore and Snow suggest, to adapt the content of current linguistic courses to meet the needs of future teachers. Unfortunately, this need is often misinterpreted as "dumbing down" material for education majors. We must overcome this barrier and make clear that we are calling for rigorous courses with high standards and relevant information.
- Most of the content specified by the AFT and by Fillmore and Snow is not included on state licensing exams or in course requirements for teachers. It is unlikely that change will occur merely because of "the current political

situation surrounding debates about bilingual education and the rather frantic search for better methods of teaching reading" that have energized Fillmore and Snow (this volume, p. 42). We must use policy levers to move the university, and state licensure requirements seem a likely place to begin. If, as appears to be the case, teacher education programs and universities more generally are going to be held accountable for the outcomes of their students,[1] and if the material we are discussing becomes part of the coursework that is required by the state and assessed by the state licensure tests, then it is probable that teacher education faculty will include the material in the teacher education curriculum.

- For the most part, teachers are educated in undergraduate school, where teacher education is often limited to the last two years of college. During those two years, the teacher education program must, at a minimum, provide candidates with the material mandated by the state for initial licensure and that required by the college for graduation—a major or a minor concentration in addition to pedagogy courses and clinical training. The content of educational linguistics is important for teachers, but we must recognize that it competes with other essential content. Instituting a 5-year teacher-training program that could accommodate more courses is improbable in the short term. Thus we must determine what educational linguistic content is crucial for pre-service education for all teachers, what is necessary for those teachers with a primary responsibility for teaching the language arts, and what must be part of continuing professional development for all teachers.

- If the content proposed by Fillmore and Snow is to be part of the education of teachers, then other content that they currently are required to learn and that faculty are currently prepared to teach must be eliminated or significantly altered to accommodate this new knowledge. The economics and politics of this statement are not trivial. The AFT has called for "funding to enable the teaching profession to reach agreement on and recommend that colleges adopt rigorous core curricula in pedagogy based on the best research into how students learn and on the content-specific teaching methods shown to be effective with students" (American Federation of Teachers, 2000a, p.8). Without that professional consensus, the university will reshape teacher education based on the predilections of some faculty members. As a result, the professional education that teachers receive will vary greatly from place to place—unlike the training in other professions—and whether they are exposed to the material called for in the AFT report or in the Fillmore and Snow chapter will remain a matter of chance.

## One Possibility

The AFT believes that the way to improve teacher preparation is to develop policies that strengthen teaching as a profession. Every prestigious profession has developed a set of broadly agreed upon understandings about the training needed for induction. It is time for the teaching profession to establish similar understandings. As the late Albert Shanker wrote,

> To be considered a true profession, an occupation must have a distinct body of knowledge—acknowledged by practitioner and consumer alike—that undergirds the profession and forms the basis of delivering high-quality services to clients. (1996, p. 220)

To that end, the National Academy of Education, in collaboration with the American Federation of Teachers, has secured funding for a project designed to identify the core content that teacher candidates should have in cognitive psychology, human development, educational assessment, and teaching strategies, particularly as they relate to language development. The project will also identify what pre-kindergarten and elementary teachers should know and be able to do to teach reading. A blue ribbon panel, co-chaired by Linda Darling Hammond and John Bransford and working in cooperation with a diverse set of teacher education institutions, will be deliberating and making recommendations with an eye to feasibility of implementation in a variety of college and university settings. The panel's meetings might provide an opportunity for the Fillmore and Snow proposal to get a fair hearing alongside the competing educational needs of pre-service teachers. It could also be the forum where a workable solution can be determined regarding the content and scope of educational linguistics that should be accommodated in undergraduate education.

# Note

[1] Title II of the Higher Education Act has reporting requirements regarding teacher education programs' effectiveness in preparing students to pass state licensure tests. If the material is incorporated into such tests, it might very well drive the curriculum of teacher education in a positive fashion.

# References

American Federation of Teachers. (1999a). *Improving reading achievement: It's union work*. Washington, DC: AFT Educational Issues Publications.

American Federation of Teachers. (1999b). *Teaching reading IS rocket science: What expert teachers of reading should know and be able to do*. Washington, DC: AFT Educational Issues Publications.

American Federation of Teachers. (2000a). *Building a profession: Strengthening teacher preparation and induction. Report of the K-16 Teacher Education Task Force*. Washington, DC: AFT Educational Issues Publications.

American Federation of Teachers. (2000b). *Doing what works: Improving big city school districts* (Educational Issues Policy Brief 12). Washington, DC: AFT Educational Issues Publications.

August, D., & Hakuta, K. (Eds.). (1997). *Improving schooling for language minority children: A research agenda*. Washington, DC: National Academy Press.

Burns, M., Griffin, P., & Snow, C. (Eds.). (1998). *Preventing reading difficulties in young children*. Washington, DC: National Academy Press.

Learning First Alliance & American Federation of Teachers. (1998). *Every child reading: An action plan*. Washington, DC: AFT Educational Issues Publications.

National Reading Panel. (2000). *Teaching children to read: An evidence-based assessment of the scientific literature on reading and its implications for reading instruction* (Reports of the subgroups. United States Department of Health and Human Services, National Institutes of Health, National Institute of Child Health and Human Development). Washington, DC: NIH Publications.

Shanker, A. (1996). Quality assurance: What must be done to strengthen the teaching profession. *Phi Delta Kappan, 78*(3), 220–224.

Snow, C., Burns, M., & Griffin, P. (Eds.). (1998). *Preventing reading difficulties in young children.* Washington, DC: National Academy Press.

# Epilogue

Catherine E. Snow
Harvard University

The paper and commentaries collected in this volume address a crucially important issue, one that has never been dealt with in any organized way in the United States. The issue is, very simply, what teachers need to know about language in order to work successfully with their students. In our original paper, which led to the development of this volume, Lily Wong Fillmore and I started with linguistic knowledge because we see it as central to the communication that is prerequisite to all teaching, and because we see it as particularly relevant to the teaching of literacy, a domain of considerable concern. In addition, of course, we are both researchers in the field of language development, so we understand the connections between linguistic knowledge and good pedagogical practice better than we understand parallel connections for knowledge of mathematics, history, and science.

The key point here, though, is that the core knowledge teachers need for any of the challenging tasks they face has never been defined and agreed upon, whether about language, pedagogy, or content. Major advances in the history of medical education came with the Flexner Report (1910), which defined the core knowledge all medical students needed to have. The immediate consequence of the Flexner Report was that many establishments that had been preparing medical doctors were closed, resulting in a temporary shortage of doctors. The long-term consequences were that medical education and the prerequisites for entry to medical school became highly consistent in content and much better in quality. Of course, the recommendations of the Flexner Report were given considerable clout by the funding support from the Carnegie Foundation for the Advancement of Teaching and the Rockefeller Foundation, which subsequently made a massive investment in promoting the recommended model.

It is difficult to imagine a Flexner-like process being undertaken for teacher education, particularly in this era of enormous teacher shortages. Perhaps a somewhat different procedure—open discussion leading to an emerging consensus—will have a similar impact. This volume is designed to contribute to such a discussion. Indeed, the paper and commentaries included here represent a model for the respectful discussion that we hope will ultimately generate consensus about what teachers need to know.

## Historical Context

When Lily Wong Fillmore and I started discussing our wish list of language-related knowledge for teacher candidates in September of 1998, we had little idea that we were entering into an existing lively national conversation. Teacher education and the knowledge base to be expected of teachers are the focus of considerably more attention, more worry, and more work than we then realized. This concern is now much more widely shared than we could have foreseen, and interest in these issues has grown over the last few years. Our small contribution to the discussion about teacher education, focusing on language-related knowledge domains, was motivated by a concern about the changing demographics of classrooms and the resultant need for teachers to understand second language acquisition and the many kinds of differences among languages. As it turns out, the specific topic of preparing teachers to work with immigrant students and other English language learners was also being thought about by Valdés (1998) and by González and Darling-Hammond (1997). Meanwhile, the superordinate topic of preparing teachers to function in urban schools was fuelling vast numbers of studies, articles, and concerns (see Weiner, 2000, for a review).

In the years since the first draft of "What Teachers Need to Know About Language" was circulated among friends, then expanded somewhat and posted to the Web, we have come to comprehend better the enormity and the ubiquity of the issues we were naively raising as if they were novel and unrecognized. Some of the expanded dimensions of these issues are suggested by the very insightful commentaries collected in this volume:

- The pressure from all sides for more time to be devoted to teacher preparation, even as the length of such programs in some places is being cut.
- The varying amounts and types of knowledge needed by teachers preparing to work with children of different ages, from different backgrounds, and in different school settings.
- The impossibility of including everything one needs to know about linguistic and cultural differences in a preservice program, thus the need to demand ongoing professional development for teachers that extends and elaborates on their preservice education after they begin teaching.
- The lack of a clear consensus on how best to ensure learning of the crucial content, whether in traditional university classrooms or in practicum settings where important aspects of teacher preparation go on.
- The difficulty of finding policy levers that would produce increased attention to educational linguistics in teacher preparation and ongoing development.

The richness of these commentaries derives from the varying perspectives of the writers, who work in the fields of early childhood education, preparation of bilingual teachers, teacher certification, teacher professional development, and teacher education. The complementarity of the various commentaries is further evidence of the broad scope of the issues raised here, as the commentators did not read each other's chapters as they wrote their own.

## Developments in Teacher Education Reform

The first draft of "What Teachers Need to Know About Language" emerged into a world where many others were thinking about related issues and making important—in some cases large-scale—efforts to address the enhancement of teacher education. Sandra Feldman's commentary mentions one of these—the establishment by the National Academy of Education (NAE), with funding from the U.S. Department of Education, of a committee to make recommendations about both the content and the design of teacher education. That committee, chaired by Linda Darling-Hammond and John Bransford, plans to produce a report in 2002. It has furthermore established a subcommittee focused specifically on the preparation of teachers to teach reading. The justification for this domain-focused subcommittee was that a widespread consensus exists about the research-informed knowledge base for teaching reading, as summarized in *Preventing Reading Difficulties in Young Children* (National Research Council, 1998) and the *Report of the National Reading Panel* (National Reading Panel, 2000). Given this consensus about what children need to know to be successful readers, and about which opportunities to learn and instructional strategies are of value in helping them become successful readers, it should be easy to define the content of teacher preparation programs.

Other past and ongoing efforts have proposed policies to bring about needed improvements in preparation to teach reading and to address the larger issue of teaching effectively in school systems characterized by significant demographic changes, raised standards, and the challenges of urban schooling. Some of these efforts are listed here.

- The establishment of the National Commission on Teaching and America's Future (NCTAF) and the issuance of its 1996 report, *What Matters Most: Teaching for America's Future.*
- A series of statements and publications issued by the American Federation of Teachers (AFT), including a resolution, *Improving Reading Achievement: It's Union Work* (1998), that endorsed the importance of professional preparation and professional development in reading for all teachers; a booklet, *Teaching Reading IS Rocket Science* (1999), which outlines domains of linguistic and orthographic knowledge that all teachers should possess; and a statement, *Building a Profession: Strengthening Teacher Preparation and Induction* (2000), focused on entrance and exit standards for teacher preparation programs and guidelines for clinical experiences and curriculum.
- The formation by the International Reading Association (IRA) of a Commission on Excellence in Teacher Education that will, among other activities, develop a description and analysis of programs designated as excellent in preparing teachers of reading, to further the work initiated by

IRA's revised *Standards for Reading Professionals* (International Reading Association, n.d.).

- Formulation of revised model standards for teacher knowledge in the domain of literacy by many states and by a number of national organizations, including the Interstate New Teacher Assessment and Support Consortium (INTASC, 1998), the National Council for Accreditation of Teacher Education (NCATE, 1999), and the Teacher Education Accreditation Council (TEAC, 2000).

- Publication by the U.S. Department of Education (1998) of a report focused on new ways to improve teacher quality.

- Enhanced attention to teacher preparation by the Carnegie Corporation of New York, which invited applications for funding to develop teacher education models (Grosso de León, 2001). The Corporation funded institutes at Harvard University and at Rutgers University at which teams from teacher education institutions and professional development efforts could work on improvement plans for their own undertakings. The Corporation has also supported the development of a consensus statement on the implications for teacher education of the "opportunity to learn" conditions identified in *Preventing Reading Difficulties in Young Children* (National Research Council, 1998) as necessary for children to become proficient readers.

- Publication by the Education Leaders Council of a report focused on teacher quality and revised certification standards (Kanstoroom & Finn, 1999).

- The establishment by the American Educational Research Association of a commission on teacher education.

- The decision by two independent study groups convened by RAND, with funding from the U. S. Department of Education, to highlight the centrality of research on teacher education within their recommendations. The groups were tasked with developing educational research agendas for mathematics and reading respectively. (See www.rand.org/multi/achievementforall for draft versions of both reports and responses to them.)

This list does not, of course, exhaust the current interest in teacher education and professional development.

If we had been aware of this high level of concern and activity when we first started talking about these issues, Lily Wong Fillmore and I would perhaps have been more apprehensive, as teacher education novices, even to enter the fray. Now that we are somewhat better informed, though, we continue to hope that there is some value to our focus on the role of learning about language in the preparation of teachers who will be encountering linguistically and culturally diverse classes and in the preparation of teachers with the responsibility for teaching reading—two groups that come close to being coextensive with the class of all teachers.

## Likely Remedies

The observation that originally motivated our writing "What Teachers Need to Know About Language"—that teacher preparation programs pay far too little attention to language—has since been confirmed. In a meeting in 2001 at Harvard University of teams from 16 teacher education programs in various universities, none of the teams reported requiring a course in educational linguistics. By the end of the institute, several had decided that developing such a course would become one of their program goals. While this is heartening, it raises the next issue—who will teach such courses? Most faculty in teacher education programs are insufficiently schooled in linguistics to do so, and faculty in linguistics departments are often not aware of the ways in which their courses would need to be adapted to demonstrate relevance to literacy and education.

The difficulty of making linguistic knowledge relevant to teachers and prospective teachers is hardly new. In 1971, the linguist Robbins Burling published an article called "Talking to Teachers About Social Dialects," in which he recounted the difficulties of making the technical aspects and the value of linguistic analysis accessible to teachers. He also described the insights that come from learning how to do so, however. Perhaps educational linguistics could constitute a model for collaboration between the faculty of education and the faculty of arts and sciences; co-teaching courses creates opportunities for both faculty members to learn new concepts, and it can provide both with opportunities to learn more about their own fields as well. Many of the changes in teacher education that are being discussed by the American Federation of Teachers, the National Academy of Education, the American

Educational Research Association, and other groups involve two main dimensions: specifying foundation skills that students should possess for entry to teacher education and greater involvement of arts and sciences faculties in both the foundational and the professional phases of teacher preparation. Educational linguistics might be a promising domain in which to work out the details of such arrangements. (See Spring, Flynn, Joseph, Moses, Steele, & Webb, 2000, for various models of introductory linguistics courses for nonlinguists.)

As the commentaries in this volume make clear, the challenge of implementing our recommendations is great. Some domains of teacher preparation are easy to divide into content knowledge and pedagogical knowledge spheres (Shulman, 2000), but for the domains of language and literacy, it is extremely hard to draw this division. Language is unlike mathematics, history, or biology—domains in which the adult's knowledge is mostly the product of instructional encounters. A native language is typically learned informally, in ways that may not generate much explicit metalinguistic or analytic knowledge. Greater metalinguistic awareness may come from learning additional languages, but in this country, the incidence of multilingualism among teachers is unfortunately quite low.

Furthermore, the scope of the knowledge about language that teachers require is broader and less well defined than for other subject matter domains, such as biology. At some levels, this knowledge is accessible to everyone because they know at least one language, but at other levels it is highly technical. A teacher needs content knowledge about language—knowledge about the existence of phonemes and morphemes, for example, or about the analysis of grammatical structure—but such knowledge is needed in order to understand children's development as learners and readers, not in order to convert it into pedagogical content to impart to the children.

Perhaps the minimum that teachers need in the domain of language is curiosity about words, a positive attitude toward linguistic analysis, and a willingness to learn about new languages. No one person knows all about the several hundred thousand words of English, nor does anyone know about the structures of all the approximately 6,000 languages and 100-plus orthographies extant in the world. Such comprehensive knowledge is not what is being suggested here.

The first benchmark en route to mastery of the domain of language for teachers should perhaps be defined as familiarity with the dimensions on which words and languages might vary and an unrelenting willingness to learn more. This level of knowledge would give teachers a basic set of tools to use to analyze new situations they encounter and a framework on which to accumulate new learning. When an English language learner struggles with a skill in reading, or when a colleague recommends speech therapy for a vernacular dialect speaker, the teacher will be able to consider the linguistic facts and form a recommendation based on them. If we could ensure that teachers graduate from their preparation programs having met that benchmark, and if we could provide professional development that responded to their willingness to learn, the quality of education enjoyed by English language learners, by speakers of vernacular dialects, and by those finding it difficult to learn to read would be improved.

In this volume, our goal has been to provoke and inform the debate on what teachers need to know about language. It is our hope that future generations of teachers will know a lot more about this foundational, yet overlooked, domain.

# References

American Federation of Teachers. (1998). *Improving reading achievement: It's union work*. AFT Convention Resolution, adopted 19 July 1998.

American Federation of Teachers. (1999). *Teaching reading IS rocket science: What expert teachers of reading should know and be able to do*. Washington, DC: Author.

American Federation of Teachers. (2000). *Building a profession: Strengthening teacher preparation and induction*. Washington, DC: Author.

Burling, R. (1971). Talking to teachers about social dialects. *Language Learning, 21*, 221-234.

Flexner, A. (1910). *Medical education in the United States and Canada*. New York: Carnegie Foundation for the Advancement of Teaching.

González, J., & Darling-Hammond, L. (1997). *New concepts for new challenges: Professional development for teachers of immigrant youth*. Washington, DC, and McHenry, IL: Center for Applied Linguistics and Delta Systems.

Grosso de León, A. (2001). Higher education's challenge: New teacher education models for a new century. New York: Carnegie Corporation of New York.

International Reading Association (n.d.). *Standards for reading professionals (revised)*. Newark, DE: Author.

Interstate New Teacher Assessment and Support Consortium. (1998). *Model standards in English language arts for beginning teacher licensing and development*. Washington, DC: Council of Chief State School Officers.

Kanstoroom, M., & Finn, C., Jr. (Eds.). (1999). *Better teachers, better schools*. Washington, DC: The Thomas B. Fordham Foundation.

National Commission on Teaching and America's Future. (1996). *What matters most: Teaching for America's future.* New York: Author.

National Council for Accreditation of Teacher Education. (1999). *Program standards for elementary teacher preparation.* Washington, DC: Author.

National Reading Panel. (2000). *Report of the National Reading Panel: Teaching children to read.* Washington, DC: National Institute of Child Health and Human Development.

National Research Council. (1998). *Preventing reading difficulties in young children.* Washington, DC: National Academy Press.

Shulman, L. (2000). Teacher development: Roles of domain expertise and pedagogical knowledge. *Journal of Applied Developmental Psychology, 25,* 129-135.

Spring, C., Flynn, M., Joseph, B., Moses, R., Steele, S., & Webb, C. (2000). The successful introductory course: Bridging the gap for the nonmajor. *Language, 76,* 110-122.

Teacher Education Accreditation Council. (2000). *Outline of a new system for the accreditation of programs in teacher education.* Washington, DC: Author.

U.S. Department of Education. (1998). *Promising practices: New ways to improve teacher quality.* Washington, DC: Author.

Valdés, G. (1998). The world outside and inside schools: Language and immigrant children. *Educational Researcher, 27,* 4-18.

Weiner, L. (2000). Research in the 90s: Implications for urban teacher preparation. *Review of Educational Research, 70,* 369-406.

# About the Authors and Editors

**Carolyn Temple Adger** directs the Language in Society Division at the Center for Applied Linguistics in Washington, DC, where she conducts research on teachers' professional discourse and on other dimensions of language in education. She is co-author or co-editor of *Kids Talk: Strategic Language Use in Later Childhood* (1998), *Dialects in Schools and Communities* (1999), and *Making the Connection: Language and Academic Achievement Among African American Students* (1999).

**Leonard Baca** is a professor of bilingual special education at the University of Colorado at Boulder. He also directs the Bueno Center For Multicultural Education. Professor Baca has directed a number of research projects on topics such as high stakes assessment for bilingual students and teacher education for bilingual students. He has also published extensively in these areas.

**Sue Bredekamp** is director of research at the Council for Early Childhood Professional Recognition and a special consultant to the Head Start Bureau. She co-authored *Learning to Read and Write: Developmentally Appropriate Practices for Young Children*, the joint position statement of the International Reading Association and the National Association for the Education of Young Children (NAEYC). She is the primary author of NAEYC's *Developmentally*

*Appropriate Practice in Early Childhood Programs*, and she has written many articles related to standards for professional practice and professional development of early childhood teachers.

**Donna Christian** is president of the Center for Applied Linguistics in Washington, DC, where she is active in research, program evaluation, policy analysis, and professional development. Her research focuses on language in education, including issues of second language learning and dialect diversity. She is co-author of *Dialects in Schools and Communities* (1999) and *Profiles in Two-Way Immersion Education* (1997) and co-editor of *Bilingual Education* (2001) and *Making the Connection: Language and Academic Achievement Among African American Students* (1999).

**Kathy Escamilla** is an associate professor at the University of Colorado at Boulder in the Division of Social, Bilingual, and Multicultural Foundations. She conducts research on educational issues related to Spanish-speaking children in U.S. public schools, particularly in the areas of second language acquisition and literacy and biliteracy development. She has published a book and more than 20 articles related to language and literacy acquisition of Spanish-speaking children in U.S. schools.

**Sandra Feldman** is president of the American Federation of Teachers and a member of the Executive Council of the AFL-CIO. Ms. Feldman is widely recognized as an authority on urban education and an advocate for children. U.S. presidents, governors, and mayors have appointed her to numerous commissions and task forces tackling educational, economic, child welfare, labor, and other social issues. Ms. Feldman was selected as one of New York City's "75 Most Influential Women" by *Crain's New York Business* and as one of the "100 Most Influential Women in America" by *Ladies' Home Journal*.

**Lily Wong Fillmore** is a professor of language, literacy, and cultural studies at the University of California at Berkeley. She has conducted a number of large studies on second language learning and the education of language minority students in California schools. She has also studied language use in native American schools and communities. Her writing on topics in language and education appears in numerous journals and books.

**Donna Gollnick** is senior vice president of the National Council for Accreditation of Teacher Education (NCATE). Formerly, she served as director of professional development at the American Association of Colleges for Teacher Education. She recently co-authored the publication, *Multicultural Education in a Pluralistic Society* (2001), which examines strategies for incorporating cultural diversity into teaching.

**Virginia Richardson** is chair of educational studies and professor of teaching and teacher education at the University of Michigan. She conducts research and publishes articles, chapters, and books on teacher education and professional development, teacher change, teacher beliefs, and the moral dimensions of classrooms. She is the editor of the recently published *Handbook of Research on Teaching* (4th ed., 2001), and of *Constructivist Teacher Education: Building a World of New Understandings* (1997).

**Catherine Snow** is the Henry Lee Shattuck Professor of Education at the Harvard Graduate School of Education. Her research interests include children's language development, literacy development, and issues related to the acquisition of English oral and literacy skills by language minority children. She has co-authored books on language development (e.g., *Pragmatic Development*, 1996) and literacy development (e.g., *Unfulfilled Expectations: Home and School Influences on Literacy*, 2000) and has published widely on these topics.

# Other Publications Available From the CALStore
## www.cal.org/store • toll-free phone 800-551-3709

### Immigrant and Refugee Populations and Education

**Access and Engagement: Program Design and Instructional Approaches for Immigrant Students in Secondary School**
  Aída Walqui

**The American Bilingual Tradition (second edition)**
  Heinz Kloss

**From the Classroom to the Community: A Fifteen-Year Experiment in Refugee Education**
  Donald A. Ranard & Margo Pfleger, Editors

**Into, Through, and Beyond Secondary School: Critical Transitions for Immigrant Youths**
  Tamara Lucas

**Literacy and Language Diversity in the United States**
  Terrence G. Wiley

**New Concepts for New Challenges: Professional Development for Teachers of Immigrant Youth**
  Josué M. González & Linda Darling-Hammond

**Through the Golden Door: Educational Approaches for Immigrant Adolescents With Limited Schooling**
  Betty Mace-Matluck, Rosalind Alexander-Kasparik, & Robin M. Queen

### English Language Education

**Cooperative Learning: A Response to Linguistic and Cultural Diversity**
  Daniel D. Holt, Editor

**English Language Learners With Special Education Needs: Identification, Placement, and Instruction**
  Alfredo J. Artiles & Alba A. Ortiz, Editors

**Making the Connection: Language and Academic Achievement Among African American Students**
  Carolyn Temple Adger, Donna Christian, & Orlando Taylor, Editors

## Foreign Language Education

**Foreign Language Assessment in Grades K–8: An Annotated Bibliography of Assessment Instruments**
Lynn Thompson

**Foreign Language Instruction in the United States: A National Survey of Elementary and Secondary Schools**
Nancy C. Rhodes & Lucinda E. Branaman

**Heritage Languages in America: Preserving a National Resource**
Joy Kreeft Peyton, Donald A. Ranard, & Scott McGinnis, Editors

**Lessons Learned: Model Early Foreign Language Programs**
Douglas F. Gilzow & Lucinda E. Branaman

**Profiles in Two-Way Immersion Education**
Donna Christian, Christopher L. Montone, Kathryn J. Lindholm, & Isolda Carranza

## Adult ESL Education

**Adult Biliteracy in the United States**
David Spener, Editor

**Approaches to Adult ESL Literacy Instruction**
JoAnn Crandall & Joy Kreeft Peyton, Editors

**Assessing Success in Family Literacy and Adult ESL (second edition)**
Daniel D. Holt & Carol H. Van Duzer, Editors

**Immigrant Learners and Their Families: Literacy to Connect the Generations**
Gail Weinstein-Shr & Elizabeth Quintero, Editors

**Making Meaning, Making Change: Participatory Curriculum Development for Adult ESL Literacy**
Elsa Roberts Auerbach

**Writing Our Lives: Reflections on Dialogue Journal Writing With Adults Learning English**
Joy Kreeft Peyton & Jana Staton, Editors

**ERIC**
Educational Resources Information Center

The Educational Resources Information Center (ERIC) is a nationwide information network that aims to improve educational practice by providing ready access to current, high-quality education literature. ERIC maintains the world's largest database of education-related materials. The ERIC database is available worldwide via the Internet and CD-ROM.

ERIC also provides direct assistance to those seeking information on education through its network of subject-specific clearinghouses, each of which offers a question-answering service and provides a wide range of free and low-cost publications on current topics in education.

The ERIC Clearinghouse on Languages and Linguistics (ERIC/CLL) collects and disseminates information related to foreign language education, the teaching and learning of English as a second language, bilingual education, and all aspects of linguistics. In addition to the *Language in Education* series, ERIC/CLL publishes a semiannual newsletter, the *ERIC/CLL News Bulletin*; a quarterly electronic newsletter, *ERIC/CLL Language Link*; a series of two-page information digests on current topics in language education; and online resource guides and directories.

ERIC/CLL is operated by the Center for Applied Linguistics, a private nonprofit organization, with funding from the National Library of Education of the U.S. Department of Education's Office of Educational Research and Improvement.

Further information on the publications, services, and other activities of ERIC/CLL can be obtained via mail, telephone, e-mail, or our Web site.

**ERIC Clearinghouse on Languages and Linguistics**
**4646 40th Street NW**
**Washington DC 20016–1859**
**800–276–9834**
**202–362–0700 ext 204**
**eric@cal.org**
**http://www.cal.org/ericcll**